"Kathryn Bonner has given us a gift for both the ordinary and crisis times of our lives. At the heart of 'Confessions' is her testimony of the need for patience, faith and love of God and family. This book will encourage you to open your heart to God, to listen to Him, and receive His love."

The Rev. Mike and Martha Wyckoff
St. Luke's on the Lake, Austin, Texas

"Kathryn is a glowing example of the message within this book. Her heartfelt confessions and sincerity in seeking to know God and to hear His voice through this interesting journey called life—will inspire you to truly hear God's whisper in every single circumstance you face."

Dr. Laura Koke,
Co-Pastor of Shoreline Christian Center in Austin,
Texas, and author of *Fit for the King*

"In what amounts to a spiritual memoir, Kathryn Bonner reflects theologically on her life's journey. She reminds the reader that there is no distinction between the "real" world and the world of the Spirit. Anyone who struggles with keeping God at the forefront day-to-day (and particularly those married to pastors) will find encouragement for the journey in this book."

The Rev. Catherine Tyndall Boyd,
Austin, Texas

"*Confessions of a Pastor's Wife: He Speaks... Can You Hear Him?* What a powerful insight into being a Pastor's wife. For years I've been one of the thousands who never thought their lives were anything but perfect. I had no idea their lives are just as real as ours. Kathryn Bonner's book is an eye-opener. I see that she walks the same path as the congregation, facing God's challenges as we all do. This book is one for the nightstand."

Leon Mentzer,
author of *Just When You Think You're All Alone*

"Kathryn is not only a dear friend; she is also my mentor and life coach. As a pastor's wife myself, I have gleaned so much from the years God has been at work in Kathryn's life and her ministry. Possessing a great gift for seeing the positive in every situation, Kathryn's story will take you from laughter to tears and is sure to move you to contemplate the greatness of our Lord Jesus Christ."

Melanie Barosh,
Wife of Worship Pastor, Crossbridge Church in Sugar Land, Texas, and mommy of two.

# Confessions
## OF A
## PASTOR'S WIFE

# *Confessions*
## OF A
## PASTOR'S WIFE

HE SPEAKS, CAN YOU HEAR HIM

KATHRYN BONNER

TATE PUBLISHING & *Enterprises*

Published by Tate Publishing & Enterprises, LLC
127 E. Trade Center Terrace | Mustang, Oklahoma 73064 USA
1.888.361.9473 | www.tatepublishing.com

Tate Publishing is committed to excellence in the publishing industry. The company reflects the philosophy established by the founders, based on Psalms 68:11,
*"The Lord gave the word and great was the company of those who published it."*

Book design copyright © 2007 by Tate Publishing, LLC. All rights reserved.
*Cover design by Jennifer R. Fisher*
*Interior design by Elizabeth A. Mason*
*Photo taken by Bruce Bonner*

Published in the United States of America

ISBN: 978-1-6046210-2-0
1. Christian Living     2. Spiritual Growth: Gener
07.08.03

# ACKNOWLEDGEMENTS

My husband, the Rev. Bruce Bonner, the love of my life! Thank you for loving me as immensely as you do! Thank you for believing in me and allowing me to be so me, for your ability to be true with yourself and with me. Your constant love is always with me.

Tabitha and KellieAnn, my precious daughters. Oh, how I love you two! I am so thankful that you two are so close to each other and for the way that we can talk about anything! What gifts you are to me. You both have taught me so much about love, living, laughter and patience and the witty ways God works! Ha!

To Gerald and Chase, thank you for loving my daughters with such precious love. Your love for them reaches out and touches my heart in ways only a parent can understand; I thank you both for that. In the years to come in your marriages, I pray you strive for all that God has for you.

Donna Garner, my mother-in-law, for teaching me the true meaning of unconditional love. You opened your heart so big and wrapped your arms around me and my girls when we came into your son's life with huge hugs, the warmest of smiles, and eyes with tears of joy as you welcomed us into your life. And you continue to do just that... you are one of the best blessings God has given me... O how I love you!

In loving memory of Rev. Robert H. Bonner, my treasured father-in-law, who was such fun for me, full of spontaneity, laughter and love!

Mom, Doris Rich, you are such a gracious writer! You have always been such a creative inspiration to me, teaching me to appreciate creativity, the written word, as well the power of my God-given dreams. The latest sonnet you have gifted me with is this...

*Dream Walk*
I henceforth step into my dreams
From whence cometh my future

Thank you for being such a dreamer, and always believing in my dreams the way you do! I love you! Thank you also for aiding in the editing of this book.

Dad, Bill Rich, you are so enjoyable always smiling, and a ray of sunshine in my life! I love your tenderness and sweet spirit. As I would read chapters over the phone to you, thank you for your compassionate tears of love as I would read. Your love for me is grand, and I am so thankful you are my Dad.

Scott and Brad Rich, my brothers, and Suzi Ziegenbein, my sister, and their families, thank you for loving me. Suzi, your prayers and love are full of excitement, laughter and passion! For each of you, "Here's to what God has just on the horizon... !"

Stan Dobbs, for being such an iron man in my life, also a true friend, even though you are my boss! Thank you for allowing me the freedom to go part-time to follow the passion of writing this book, for understanding what it means to be called by God to something and sharing in that joy with me. Your love for God is truly what motivates you, and all who know you know this about you.

Thank you, Mary MacGregor, for being such a powerful, yet graceful angel that the Lord has provided in our life. I love the way you love God!

In honor and memory of The Right Reverend Leo Alard, who felt every thing with such passion and who championed us with a passion you don't see in most human beings! I have an entire chapter in this book about the way the Lord used him in our lives so profoundly!

With love, appreciation and great thanks to Melanie Barosh, Kati Smith, Suzi Raines, Tammie Brown, and Julie Polansky, my precious friends who have prayed continuously with and for me during the entirety of this book. Big love hugs all around! I am so grateful to each of you.

Thanks to my Apartment Life family, to each of you who have prayed and cheered me on during this process! A few that I want to thank in particular for your prayers: Keri Fruend, Tina Hansen, Wes Hood, Terri Jones, and Connie Settlemoir.

To my Wednesday Morning Reunion Prayer Group, Nancy Wren, Jan Halstead, and Fran Hart—you girls I love! Thank you for getting so excited with me, praying for me, listening to me, and all the while lifting me up to the Most High God. I have intensely felt your prayers, praising God for each of you with arms lifted up!

To my dear friend, Patty Craig, who not only gives fully of herself in love and wisdom but in addition donated her loving heart and razor-sharp editing eyes to this book. Thank you! You are truly a gift to both Bruce and me in more ways than could ever be catalogued here.

To Elsa Humphries, whose love and passion for life and the Lord thrill me, and so does your friendship! For the love, prayers, and support you have given me throughout the years, and in the aid of editing. I remain grateful for all you bring to my life.

For my church family at Christ Church, and my precious girlfriends who have walked alongside me as this book was birthed. They have shared my awe of this thing really happening, listened to me struggle, share in my amazement with God through it all. Thank you for listening to me ramble, for praying with and for me, for being excited for me, for finding out more about me and loving me anyway. I praise God for my sweet friends!

Much thanks to Joan Webb, my first coach who really caused me to believe that this book was a possibility and encouraged me to obey God's calling upon my life, to step out in faith hand in hand with the Lord, encouraging me to write this book. Wow! You are a true coach in every sense of the word!

Kellie Gotthardt, who so randomly brought me to Joan Webb, but for a totally different reason. Who knew? God did! Another one of those crazy, wonderful Holy Spirit connections!

To Gisele Fernandez, my wonderful coach who was with me when I received my letter of acceptance from Tate Publishing and my certification from CTI as a professional life coach! Thanks for pushing me, never letting me wiggle away from this book, and for constantly holding me accountable. Thanks also for reminding me to keep leaning into this wonderful big place of "walking with full-size faith!"

A big thank you to several of my coaching friends across the globe who have been champions, cheerleaders and coaches along the way! As we coaches say, "I am complete!"

And first and foremost, Yahweh, My Lord, my God, Adonay, my Savior, King of Kings, Aba, Creator of the Universe, El Shadday, I have drawn closer to you by being obedient to you in the writing of this book. I have leaned on you in my own personal doubts, been carried by your big faith in me and love for me in ways I have not experienced before. How I love you, my Lord, and I pray that all humankind, Your great creation, fall in love with You, too.

# TABLE OF CONTENTS

# INTRODUCTION

*I* want to share with you that I have never had an aspiration to write a book. I am not one who journals often, although I do from time to time, and while doing so have always seemed to find the answers to many of the questions I have for God. It is as though He is answering all of my questions for me while I write. This is the Holy Spirit in action. I love the way the Holy Spirit works! You would think that I would journal more often simply for that reason alone. I can allow the busyness of every day get in the way of doing the things that God has for me to do even though I know they are good for me.

I have been *told* to write this book. Yes, I did say *told* to write it. This book came into being because of a very profound experience I had with God.

I was sitting on the sofa in the den on a Wednesday evening watching TV. I couldn't even tell you what show I was watching when all of a sudden all of these chapter titles came pouring into my head! I literally ran into my office and grabbed my prayer journal and wrote them all down as swiftly as they were coming. There were over twenty chapter titles! It was such a profound experience, I couldn't do much in that moment except stand there staring at the page wondering what just happened. As I stood there staring, I understood that these would be the chapters titles in a book, a book He was *telling* me to write! As I read each chapter title, I knew what was going to be in every single chapter! I knew what was to be written. It was amazing! Another thing I need to share with you is the rapid speed in which the list of chapter titles came, and yet, the Lord gave them to me in "perfect speed"—no faster than I could write so that I wouldn't forget any of them! When He gives, He gives so perfectly!

In retrospect I looked at this as my "burning bush event." It's not as *though* God had spoken to me, He *actually did speak to me, telling* me to write this book for Him. I imagine that I felt much like Moses did! I felt overwhelmed, unable, unqualified, and unworthy. Because I felt all of those things, I set my prayer journal on the shelf in my office and left it there for a few months. God would cause me to remember it, having my mind race back to the many chapter titles. Again I would feel unable, and unqualified to attempt to tackle this book. I recognized that was God calling me back to it, encouraging me to live into the BIG assignment that He had given me. He wanted me to embrace it, to experience the joy of it rather than the fear of it. I began to consider small thoughts like, *"Maybe I can do this! Maybe He will continue to guide me through it. He has always been my guide before. Why would he stop now?"* I thought other thoughts like,

*"Kathryn, you of all people, being a life coach, have*

*always been the one to step out in faith. You have always allowed the Spirit to lead you rather than fear. Haven't you always said this to others you coach when they have felt afraid, when they knew that God was calling them to something? Practice what you preach, girl! Step out in faith."*

I want to give you hope and joy in your journey. The choice to live in every moment with love, faith and glorious expectation is mine and yours! Don't let anything or anyone (not even yourself) stop you from living into the glory that the Lord has planned for you. For those of you who have dreams, keep dreaming, push beyond the limits of your comfort zone! Do you realize who gave you those dreams? Do you trust in the one who gave them to you? Step out in faith, don't just sit there sitting on your dream; rather than squash it, embrace it! Love it, and live it!

God speaks to me, and He speaks to you. He gives us these things to do because He believes in us even when we don't believe in ourselves! God wants you to live into His will, because His will for us is first-rate!

I write this book to several different audiences, for laity, clergy, clergy spouses, and for those who need hope. I want to share with you that living in the midst moment by moment in the "joy of the Lord" is a choice. What will you choose? It all boils down to the choices you make; it's really simple when you think of it like that.

Blessings to you as you read and choose to live out your life in total faith! You will never ever regret it...

Shhhh.... Listen! He is speaking to you now... can you hear Him?

# DISCOVERING GOD

*Even in our youth we knew that our
Creator was amazing.*

*I* was alone, and scared. Only nineteen, so young. So afraid.

This can't be true! Oh God! Oh God! NO! NO! Please God, NO! Please don't let me be pregnant! Oh my God! Is this really happening to me? Oh God, please, please don't let this be happening to me! I can't do this!

I'd been living on my own since I was seventeen years old, almost eighteen. Just before graduating from high school, I'd registered for college, had a job at an apartment community as a leasing agent. One of the benefits was a free apartment which I was ecstatic about. Being out on my own, living the life of a full fledged adult, what wonderful freedom!

Should I tell him I'm pregnant? What would he say? Would he want to get married? Do I want to marry him? No! I don't want to marry him! I really don't! This is not what I want! I was so frightened, and so alone, longing for the days of being a young girl without a care in the world when my friends and I would spend hours sky gazing.

*I believe that God uses His incredible creation as one of the many ways to reveal Himself to us. He wants to make sure that we don't miss the opportunity to know Him.*

Oh Lord, I don't want to be here! How did I get here??!! Where are you God?! Are you here with me? Oh God, I'm panicking here, I need you, Lord! Oh Lord, take me back to those days of no worry; take me back to the honeysuckle bushes under the sky...

Do you remember as a child of eight or nine years old looking up into the majestic, infinite sky and seeing all kinds of things in the clouds? When I was a young girl, my friends and I would lie in the grass, flat on our backs, gazing up at the wispy clouds blowing into different shapes. We watched as they would ever so slowly be blown, forming countless shapes. We'd point up to the clouds and ask one another, "Do you see the poodle? Do you see the airplane? Do you see the witch?... the high heel shoes?... the car?... the camel?... the pelican?" Some of us would immediately see the object, and some of us would struggle trying to see what the clouds reflected. Then they would mutate into totally new-fangled shapes as the breeze gently blew, our imagination waiting to see what was to be created next. We'd lie there for hours on beautiful days. Even in our youth we knew that our Creator was amazing. Lying there with friends, we would have really deep and profound conversations for our age, looking up at the vast, never-ending blue and white puffs in the sky, we'd ask such powerfully felt questions wondering, "How in the world did God form the earth and everything in it?"

> He wraps himself in light as with a garment; He stretches out the heavens like a tent and lays the beams of his upper chambers on their waters. He makes the clouds his chariot and rides on the wings of wind.
>
> Psalm 104:2–3 NIV

I believe that God uses His incredible creation as one of the many ways to reveal Himself to us. He wants to make sure that we don't miss the opportunity to know Him.

As we would lie there sky gazing, there was a huge, sweet-smelling honeysuckle bush that lined an entire fence, and we'd pick the golden yellow, trumpet-shaped flower off of the bush and find the little green stem on the end and pull it like a thread through the flower, dragging the little tiny dab of sugary sweet syrup to our lips and enjoy the taste of the sweet honey. We wondered how the sweet syrup got in the beautiful honeysuckle flower. Again we were amazed with the Lord's creative intelligence. Continuing to survey the clouds while enjoying the sweet taste of honeysuckle, we delighted in the amazement and wonder of it all! This was the way that I began to attempt to discover who and what God was. As we surveyed our surroundings, the talk would inevitably shift to God.

> *Ultimately, I hear and experience God through love, which I consider to be the most creative and intelligent source.*

Every now and then as we were lying there, our ears heard the buzzing sound of a bumblebee, and we'd look around in a bit of fright, our eyes following it. The bumblebee is an amazing creature. Did you know it is one of the few insects that can regulate body temperature through both solar radiation (radiant energy emitted by the sun) and through an internal mechanism of cooling from their abdomens? God's creation is truly incredible to me!

We would then fix our eyes on other creatures around us. We'd pick up the roly-polies bugs (also known as pill bugs, and armadillo bugs). These bugs have a shell-like body that can tuck and roll up for protection, which is how they got many of the names we called them. Most people think that they are insects, but they are not. They actually breathe through gills! In the tiniest little creature, there is such creativity, such beauty!

Early on in my life I became aware of the Holy Spirit through God's creation, through the wind and rain, through the flowing river, through silence and music, through laughter and tears, through joy and relationships, through sweet aromas, sunrises and sunsets, and clouds. Ultimately, I hear and experience God through love, which I consider to be the most creative and intelligent source!

> O Lord, our Lord, How majestic is Your name in all the earth! You have displayed Your splendor above the heavens!
>
> Psalm 8:1 NASB

## As a Teenager...

A few years later when I was fourteen years old, I'd gone to a week long summer camp with my youth group. It was an amazing place! It was a week overflowing with countless new experiences in Christ. I had never "*felt*" the powerfulness of God the way I did that week at camp. This was the very first point in time that I had ever known *for sure* that God was *actually real!* It was overwhelming, it was powerful, it was pure. There was no question for me; God was *REAL* and I wanted to have Him become the Lord of my life!! I prayed for Him to forgive me, to come into my heart, and make Him the Master of my life! I cried tears of joy, tears of realization! I knew that this was something true, something amazing and I knew that the Lord was going to be active in my life! This is really the first time I chose to walk with God. I went back to high school and tried to live for Him. It was hard, as I had to back away from the crowd I was hanging out with. I had begun to act out in ways that I shouldn't have. My parents were going through a divorce, and we lived with my mother. With the lack of parental involvement due to my parents' divorce, I ventured off into some areas I should not have gone. I was headed down the wrong path. It is amazing how we can get hooked into things so quickly. I tried to detach myself from the "old group" and latch onto a new group. The kids in the group I'd been hanging out with didn't want to let me go. It was a difficult period for me. Peer pressure is such a difficult thing! I went to my mother and told her that I needed to embark on a new walk, explaining the situation to her.

If we live by the Spirit, let us also walk by the Spirit.

Gal 5:25 NASB

> *How many times in our lives do we try to make God responsible for our own actions and choices?*

I needed to go to a different school. She agreed and put the house on the market and we moved. That was such an amazing gift that my mother gave to me. She sold her dream house. It was also financially good for her at the time to scale down, because of the house payments. So she sold the house, and we moved into a new neighborhood and a new school district.

The new neighborhood we moved to had several of the kids from my youth group living there as well. That was a real blessing for me! I knew that my mom was making a sacrifice for me as well. Being an adult now with grown children of my own, I can appreciate it so much more than I could then. I began my sophomore year at the new school, adopting better friends and a better way of living, staying out of trouble.

### Forgetting my Lord, and leaving Him behind...

Oddly enough, over a period of the next few years I seemed to have forgotten about my Lord. Even though all of this change in my life had come about because of Him, I didn't make Him the Lord of my life. I was definitely hanging out with much better kids and staying out of trouble. I had made a productive change, and was having heaps of fun, but I wasn't making an effort to forge the relationship with God I had intended to. I really didn't have the direction I needed. I was unsure of how to develop and nurture that relationship.

It wouldn't be until my twenties that I would turn back to my Lord. Of course, I prayed every now and then, and thought about God primarily when I had a need. But overall I wasn't really focused on, or into, God anymore. Yes, I was a believer, just not living my life for Him.

### Are you there, God? I could really use you right about now...

I'm so scared, God, I'm so scared! If you can make this not be true, I promise, God, I promise to really follow you now! Please, God, please, I'm praying to you now, God. I'm desperate for you! Don't leave me here! Don't let this be happening to me, God! I don't want to be pregnant! Take this from me, Lord!

How many times in our lives do we try to make God

responsible for our own actions and choices? How often do we attack Him for our misdoing? Why do we expect Him to take the blame for our actions!? How many times do we ask Him to make it go away?

> *Until we know Christ, we cannot know ourselves fully.*

Until we grow up spiritually we will never have our heart's desire. Once our heart's desire becomes His heart's desire, then and only then will we experience the full joy that we search for.

Until we know Christ, we cannot know ourselves fully. When we fail to know Him in a deep personal way; really get to know Him through His word, then we fail to know who He created us to be.

The Lord can always take our mess and use it as a message for His glory. He truly wants the very best for us. He can take anything and bring restoration, and beautify it in such a way that everyone looking at it sees His reflection. Oh I thank you, Lord, for that!

I knew I had to call my mom. I had so much shame and so much fear. Before dialing her number I said a quick prayer for strength and swallowed hard. The phone rang. I hung up. God, I can't do this! Oh God, please, make this go away! I sat with my hand still on the phone; I shook my hands in a nervous frenzy, trying to shake the nervousness out of them. I cried with shame, curling up in a ball next to the phone.

I began to think about my brothers and what they would think of their sister. Oh, how I didn't want to let them down! My little sister, how she looked up to me and how ashamed I would be to look at my sweet little sis. I would be such a shame for my dad to see. I would be too embarrassed to face him. Though I knew none of them would say anything ugly to me, I knew in my heart the sadness and shame I would bring them. They were such great kids; they were all so good. I knew that I'd be bringing them such shame. Oh God, if I could keep this a secret that only you and I would know... please, God!

Oh God, I beg you! Please God, make this miraculously disappear! You can, God, if you really wanted to you could! You are all powerful, right? Do this for me, Lord! I promise I'll be good; I'll change. Please, God, I'm begging you! I cried out with tears so big, and a heart so wrought with fear and anguish that I can not even begin to describe.

Do you love me, Lord? If you do, please make this go away! Do you love me, Lord?

After many hours of struggle, I go back to the phone, and dial my mom. It rings. I force myself to stay on the line and wait for her to answer. She does.

"Hello."

"Mom?"

"Yes."

"It's me, mom, Kathryn."

"Yes, I know. Are you alright?"

"No, mom, I'm not; I have a big problem, and I

don't know what to do." I am trying to keep it together, no tears, just the facts, staying strong.

"What's the problem?"

---

*The Lord can always take our mess and use it as a message for His glory.*

---

"I don't know how to tell you except to just tell you; I'm pregnant and I don't know what to do."

Silence... a very *loud* silence!

"Are you there, mom?"

"Yes, I'm here."

"Say something."

"I'm thinking."

"Well, what do you think? Do you hate me?"

"No, Kathryn, of course not. I could never ever hate you. You know that. I love you, Kathryn."

I begin to cry tears of thanks. Thanks that she still loves me, thanks that I'm not hated, thanks that I told my mom. Thanks that she isn't yelling at me, thanks that she is here with me in that moment of my most fearful place. Thanks to God for giving me the strength to make the call.

"How far along are you?"

"I'm not sure, about three months I think."

"Do you love him?"

Silence...

"Kathryn, do you love him?"

"Yes, but not the kind of love to be married to him."

"Well, it looks like you're going to have to get married anyway. You can make it a Valentine's Day wedding." She said it so matter-of-factly.

"I guess I could." I begin to shut down, and just give in to it. There doesn't seem to be any other way out.

Wedding plans were started immediately, and I was married that Valentine's Day, turned twenty in June, and Tabitha was born in July, 1982. Kellie Ann, our second child, was born in March of 1985. The marriage lasted seven years. The last year of the marriage we were separated. I was married to a man with a good heart; however, I later learned that he was seriously plagued with drug addictions. Throughout the years I knew that there was something wrong, yet I didn't realize the severity until the last few years of our marriage. At first I believed that I would be able to change him, learning later the sad and painful realization that I alone cannot change anyone; he has to be willing to change. In the end, sadly, the addiction came first, before me, before the girls, and before God.

*Realizing the need for God and seeking out my Lord....*

Jesus said, "You're not listening. Let me say it again. Unless a person submits to this original creation—the "wind hovering over the water' creation, the invisible moving the visible, a baptism into a new life—it's not possible to enter God's kingdom.

John 3:5 MSG

> *I began to cry tears of thanks.*

The above Scripture passage is so profound! Read it once again.

Do you understand how powerful and profound those words are? What do you glean from them? How often are we not listening? How often does the Lord God take the time to repeat Himself to us? I am SO appreciative that our Lord repeats Himself to us time and time again! Sometimes, we are what I call "repetitive learners." It would be nice if we got it the first time! I yearn to live here and now in God's kingdom! I long to live fully into the new life He has for me! Think about what it means to submit to the original creation—the "wind hovering over the water" creation, the invisible moving the visible, a baptism into a new life. What a picture of strength and majesty and mystery and holiness! We have this kind of Creator wanting us to be in connection with Him!

So many of us given the opportunity would jump at the chance to be in the presence of Oprah. To be able to hang out with her, we all think of it from time to time, don't we? We all think if I just had the chance to know her, my life would be so much better. My dreams would be answered. Yes, she's a wonderful woman, a woman who I believe is a change agent for the world, used by God.

But let me tell you, to be in complete connection with the Almighty is where you and I should long to be!

Look at the ability He has... *the invisible moving the visible,* a *baptism into new life.* This is where you want to be, my friends, hanging out with Him!

A few years before the marriage was over, I began to seek out my Lord, to start hanging out with Him if you will. I longed for Him to be present in my life. I had a real need for Him and began to discover Him in the small "Ah ha's" of living.

As I began to experience Him again, I found it to be very refreshing. And it was a renewal; it was new life just as the Scripture above promises! I began to experience His love for me in many unexpected ways. The Lord began to position godly girlfriends in my life. They prayed with me and for me during my struggling marriage. His presence around me was unmistakable, unwavering and unshakable.

I was separated, and the divorce had been filed. It was just me and my two little girls on our own and with God's help, we were making it! We were going to church together each Sunday. I wanted them to be on familiar and intimate terms with the Lord growing up. I wanted to be re-connected to the love I'd known in Christ Jesus at the age of fourteen. So we went on our church search. Finding the perfect church for all three of us wasn't happening quickly. We pursued it until we found it.

I was satisfied, at ease with my life, and the three of us girls were having fun together. I was not looking to be in a new relationship. I didn't want men coming in and out of my home because of my daughters. I didn't want to expose them to that. We were commencing our walk of faith.

Little did I know where this walk was going to take me, but God knew...

## Another new beginning!

---

*His presence around me was unmistakable, unwavering, and unshakable!*

---

Isn't it amazing how our Lord brings us to so many new beginnings in this wonderful life?

So if you're serious about living this new resurrection life with Christ, act like it. Pursue the things over which Christ presides. Don't shuffle along, eyes to the ground, absorbed with the things right in front of you. Look up, and be alert to what is going on around Christ—that's where the action is. See things from his perspective.

Colossians 3:1 MSG

As I write I find myself thinking about beginnings. Hmmm... where should I start? Perhaps for me the best place to start is when Bruce and I met, although I am in another new beginning stage of my life now as I write. It's so interesting the way God gives us new beginnings at the different stages of our lives. So wonderful and so full of wonder!

I'll start with when I met Bruce. Oh, how I give thanks for the love of my life! Bruce and I met on March

29, 1989. I had been separated for about a year, going through a difficult divorce. I was not dating, nor was I interested in dating (having my two little girls, Tabitha, age six, and Kellie Ann, age four) at that particular time. I wasn't going to be bringing men in and out of my life. I was happy with it just being my two angels and me. The fun we had was great! I felt so complete with them. I really felt like it would be just the three of us from here on out, and I was at total peace with that.

Well, the day came when Ray (one of the residents) came into my office. He asked me out. I explained to him that I could not date the residents. He then asked me what kind of man I was looking for. Embarrassed and feeling a little awkward, I said I wasn't looking. Ray persisted and asked the question a little differently in hopes of a new response. He said, "If you *were* looking, what would you be looking for?"

I thought it was kind of humorous and obliged him with a long list of qualities sort of like this..."Well, he must be tall, dark hair, nice thick hair, good looking, non-smoker, non-drinker, first and foremost he MUST have Christ as the center of his life, good sense of humor, financially secure, great with kids, treat me like a queen..." and then I said, "Obviously there isn't a man alive who could fill the bill!" I laughed and thought that would be the end of it. It was obvious to Ray that he didn't fit the bill except for the fact that he was tall, dark, and good-looking. I laughed and passed it off, not thinking anymore about it.

> *Little did I know where this walk was going to take me, but God knew...*

Two days later Ray came back into my office and said, "I think I have found the guy for you!" I looked at him as if he were crazy! He said, "No, really! Why don't you go out with us one evening?" I was thinking to myself, *"Are you crazy? I am not going anywhere, especially on a date at night!"*

I spoke up and said, "No, not at night, I'm just not comfortable with that, because of my girls."

He responded with another solution saying, "Okay, well how about lunch?" I thought to myself, *"This is great; only an hour out of my day. I don't have to be stuck with them for several hours, and I would have to get back to work."*

I said, "Okay, that sounds good. Where would you all like to go?"

He said, "Do you like Chinese?"

I said, "Yes, I love it!"

He said, "Okay, we will pick you up."

Here I go thinking, *"I don't want to be alone with these guys,"* so I say quickly and firmly, "No, I'll meet you there. When and what time?"

We set the time for noon next week on March 29, at the Hunan Lion Chinese Restaurant in Round Rock. I wrote it down in my Day Timer so that I would not forget.

The day of March 29 arrived, and I had completely forgotten about all of it. I was at my desk and just happened to look down at my Day Timer and noticed that I had lunch scheduled at noon to meet Ray and Bruce! Oh my gosh, I'm SO late!! Even though I really wasn't interested in meeting them for lunch, I have to admit that I still wanted to look great! I really hadn't remembered it at all. I had rather long hair at the time, and I had put it up in a bun that day. Who wants to meet a guy for the first time with your hair in a "librarian's bun"?! I had this really ugly, really, really baggy red dress on, too! I told my staff that I had a lunch appointment and ran out the door to meet them.

By the time I arrived, the guys had already ordered and were eating. They thought that they were being stood up. I apologized and sat down to eat with them. I felt kind of frenzied, and I am sure that they were thinking what a ditsy girl! I honestly don't remember any of the conversation at the meal. I really don't. Sometimes I try really hard to recall it, and I simply cannot pull any memories. I can remember some of my thoughts about my impression of Bruce, and they went something like this..."Wow, he's short, and doesn't have very thick hair, but he seems nice, and has a great sense of humor." The only conversation I do remember is while we were standing at the door of the restaurant. Ray was paying for the meal, and Bruce and I were standing back together in idle chit chat. Then Bruce asked me for my phone number, and I gave it to him. He also gave me his (but I knew in the back of my mind that I wouldn't be calling him).

Two days later my phone rang, and it was Bruce. We visited for a good amount of time, and I remember thinking that he seemed nice enough. Bruce called me again the next evening, and we talked on the phone for several hours. It was peculiar that we could converse so easily about so much! He knew that my divorce was to be final in two weeks. I didn't speak much about any of that to him.

> *I love the way the Lord has used dreams throughout the Bible. He has given us a few along the way that I've never forgotten.*

We went out on another lunch date and continued to speak on the phone a lot. My divorce was final, but there was still some difficulty, some very trying things going on that I did not share with Bruce.

During this time I was managing an apartment community, and we had to provide the residents with a courtesy patrol. I'd hired a Texas Ranger to fill that position, and he lived at the property. His apartment was diagonal to mine. As the divorce became more difficult, I shared the tribulations with this friend. It was as though God had provided me with a protector. Bruce and I joked that he had probably run a thorough background check on Bruce! God really did provide for me during this time. He never leaves us or forsakes us! I shared with my friend what was going on, and he put a tap on my phone so that we could get all of this to stop. He asked me if I had shared all of the trouble I was going through with Bruce.

I hadn't because I really didn't know him very well and didn't want to drag him into it. He advised me to tell Bruce, that I needed to level with him. Taking his advice, I called Bruce that evening to let him know and told him that it probably wasn't a good idea that I see him anymore, that we should let it go, explaining how rough things were at the time. Bruce understood, and we hung up the phone for what I thought would be for good.

Thirty minutes later the phone rang! Bruce explained to me that he had really been thinking about this dilemma. He didn't want my ex-husband to be able to dictate my life or his. We talked more, and he asked me why I hadn't told him about all of the stuff going on and I explained. Bruce prayed with me right then and there over the phone. I began to feel the peace of our Lord immediately. It moved me so deeply that he prayed with me. If I was going to get into another relationship, it was going to be Christ-centered; I wasn't going to have it any other way. I loved it that I didn't have to ask him to pray, I loved it that it was such a part of who Bruce was. It was such a part of who I was. God drew us closer to each other over the phone that night. I began to feel safe with Bruce on many levels, emotionally, and spiritually.

Prayer is really how we started out together. We continued to pray together in every phone conversation.

*DREAMS~ there have been several that have played a very important part in mine and Bruce's lives. I will share a few of them. I love the way the Lord has used dreams throughout the Bible. He has given us a few along the way that I've never forgotten.*

At the time my mother lived in Missouri, and I

would call her and talk to her about Bruce. She would get excited with me, and she also cautioned me. I had in fact dreamt about him before I ever met him, and she reminded me of the dream...

---

*Invite our Lord to be present together
in your relationship.*

---

### The Dream ~

Several months prior to meeting Bruce I had this amazing dream. I was in a gorgeous meadow with gently sloping hills; the grass was a soft lush green. Flowers were in bloom, rabbits were jumping about. There were several stone cottages around us, with cobblestone sidewalks leading up to them. Beautiful rose bushes, flower gardens, much like the English flower gardens you see in photos. The cottages were hundreds of years old. . It was the most picturesque story book scene. I was lying on my stomach on the lawn with the puffs of wind gently blowing through my hair. There was a man sitting beside me on the ground, he was softly stroking my hair, gazing adoringly into my eyes. His love is genuine; his countenance is peaceful and trusting. He is my best friend, and he is my husband. I know him as perfect for me and a gift from God.

### Our First Date ~

On our first actual evening date, Bruce told the

babysitter that he was going to marry me! I just laughed it off, but he really meant it. It was funny because when we would talk on the phone, I could talk about anything with him, but when I saw him in person I would become very shy. I was nervous because I was beginning to feel very deeply about him.

We talked on the phone more than we saw each other because he lived in South Austin, and I lived in Round Rock (just north of Austin), and he was taking classes at night working toward obtaining his degree.

There were many things that we prayed about, our emotions, our fears, and our excitement. Prayer was how we really started out in our relationship. It's the way you invite our Lord to be present together in your relationship. I truly believe that ALL Christian couples should be praying TOGETHER every single day! Yes, you definitely need your *own* prayer time with the Lord daily but you also need your time *together* to pray. This always keeps God in the very center of your relationship. It's just not healthy not to do this. Each morning that we pray together we experience SO much more!

I had reserved a spot at a spiritual retreat long before I met Bruce for that June. I was really looking forward to the retreat and to drawing nearer to the Lord. I needed it. One evening in May, Bruce took me out to dinner, and I told him that I was going to be gone for a week on the retreat, and he asked if he could go. I, for some reason, didn't take him seriously and just said, "Sure, that would be fine."

Bruce was working at Bergstrom Air Force Base as a civilian and was also a reservist. He was going to be headed out of town for TDY (a short assignment overseas) for two weeks in June. I would be leaving for my retreat the day after he was to return. Just before he was to leave, he asked me if I found out if there was any availability for him to go on the retreat. I explained that I didn't check into it, that I didn't really think he was serious. He explained that he was serious, so reservations were made for him.

> *Neither of us was sure about exactly where God was going to take us, but we both knew He had a call on our lives.*

My birthday was June 3, and he left June 4 for TDY. For my birthday he bought me a gold rose with a diamond in the center on a gold chain. I love it to this day! He also made one of those "tree trunk" clocks and glued letters on it that said "Bruce & Kathryn." Things must me getting serious! I was really going to miss him when he was gone.

I made a goody box for him to take. I packed it with several kinds of homemade cookies (and I don't even cook!!). I went and bought a card for each day that he was there and labeled them Mon. Tues. Wed. etc., so that he would know when to open each one.

Little did I know that he had done the same thing! He had purchased all of the cards and was having a gal mail them out so that I would have a card arriving every day that he was gone. He also sent me roses!

The day after he was back, we got in his Bronco and drove the twelve hour drive to Missouri. On the drive there we were having a great time talking and dreaming. About eight or nine hours into the drive, he told me that he loved me and wanted to marry me! All kinds of bells and whistles were going off in my head! All of a sudden I was stressed out! I was going there for peace, for a time of rest and renewal which I desperately needed! I looked at him and said, "Bruce, my intent for coming here was for relaxation, for peace, and to get closer to the Lord. Please don't ask me that again because this really stresses me out!" Silence... for quite awhile.

In retrospect, I laugh at that response! It probably wasn't the best way to respond, but I honestly wasn't expecting it; nor was I even close to being ready for a proposal!

We continued to drive to our peaceful destination. I knew that he was hurt, *but that would not be any reason for me to say yes to his proposal. How many times do we say yes to things we should be saying no to, just because we don't want to hurt someone's feelings?*

At the retreat several days passed...

We heard many speakers over the next few days. We met so many wonderful people. We spent a lot of great time together. I was truly falling in love with Bruce!

During one of the evenings there, we both began to share how we felt God had been calling us into ministry. Both of us were considering seminary. Neither of us was sure about exactly where He was going to take us, but we both knew He had a call on our lives. Bruce began feeling the call at the age of twelve. I was just beginning to feel it in the last year, but it was strong!

## The ACTION of the DREAM

After being there for about five days, we were sitting in a beautiful rose garden with little rabbits hopping around. It was so beautiful, the weather was perfect, and the sweet aroma of the roses was everywhere. We were sitting on a bench talking and holding hands when Bruce got down on bended knee in front of me and told me how much he loved me and couldn't imagine life without me and asked me to marry him, to be his wife! I looked down into his gorgeous brown eyes that had tears in them and saw a man who truly loved me and whom I truly loved! I began to weep tears of joy and said, "Yes, of course I will marry you, I would be a fool not to! I love you!" We hugged and laughed and cried! It was a whirlwind romance!

> _Prayer is powerful and through it, grace abounds, forgiveness flows, joy radiates._

On the twelve hour ride back to Austin/Round Rock, we planned the wedding. We set the date and many of the details.

Bruce and I met on March 29, 1989, and we were married on August 26, 1989—five months and we were married! It has been wonderful. He continues to be my very best friend. He is my love!

Regard your relationships with whomever you are dating as time to completely rely on the Lord for your wisdom and guidance. I made the mistake of not doing that with my first marriage. Place the Lord first in your life, in every area, not just some of the areas but in every area! This will allow for you to know His will for you. Root all things in prayer, even the smallest of things. God always guides us with His perfect wisdom and direction. We are Holy Spirit driven; we need to come to that understanding as quickly as possible. When we do understand this, we allow His Holiness to guide and direct our path. Prayer is powerful and through it, grace abounds, forgiveness flows, joy radiates.

# LEARNING TO DRIVE AT AGE THIRTY-TWO

---

*We wanted our daughters to know what a truly good marriage was, and the only way for them to do so was to witness it.*

On this highway of life as you learn to drive, I pray that when you get turned around and sometimes feel lost, you find your way back to the place that God is leading you.

Now Jesus himself was about thirty years old when he began his ministry. He was the son, so it was thought, of Joseph...

Luke 3:23 NIV

*Jesus in His earthly role grew up in a blended family... Joseph is a role model for all dads, as he embraced his God-given son, Jesus.*

The verse above speaks so beautifully. It says so much, even though it doesn't go into great detail about how Joseph came to be the father of Jesus. I love it when it says, *"so it was thought* of Joseph."* This is saying that many of the people thought that Joseph was the biological father of Jesus. We know that there were a select few, primarily family and friends, who knew the details, but most did not. Jesus was raised with an amazing father in Joseph, who was obviously hand-picked by God. I believe that Bruce was hand-picked by God to raise my girls along with me. For me it wasn't easy to trust another man in the raising of my girls. God trusted Joseph; I trusted Bruce.

Joseph was the earthly father of Jesus; he had the huge job to be the earthly father of the Son of God! God had to trust Joseph to do so. In Matthew Chapter 1, Joseph is described as a righteous man. Joseph knew that this child was not of his own flesh, yet he also knew that the child had been entrusted to his care. What I admire about what the Scripture reveals to us is the humanness of Joseph. In Matthew, Chapter 1, it tells us that at first Joseph broke off his engagement with Mary and was going to quietly divorce her. The realization of her pregnancy, knowing that it could not be his own child, had to have hurt him deeply. This was certainly not how he'd originally envisioned his life with Mary.

After the angel came and visited Joseph, a supernatural light was shed on the situation, causing him to be obedient to what the angel had said. Joseph had to be a man of integrity, honor, and innate goodness to be chosen as the one to raise the Son of God. I believe that Joseph had to be a man of strong character in order to get through the harsh judgments and rumors of the people that were to come his way. This is probably one of the reasons that the Lord God chose him to raise Jesus. In the book of Matthew he is described as a righteous man.

Much like Joseph (what he originally thought would be was not to be), the same was true for Bruce. I was not on Bruce's ideal list of who he thought he wanted to marry. I was one who'd been divorced, and one with two children. He envisioned himself starting marriage in the *traditional sense.* God had other plans for Bruce.

Jesus in His earthly role, grew up in a blended family. Joseph is a role model for all dads, as he embraced his God given-son, Jesus. Bruce has always said that "All children are gifts–given by God, no matter how they come to you."

Of course, I am no Mary, and Bruce is no Joseph, but I love the blended family in Mary, Joseph and Jesus.

> *I encourage you to give your truth to God, no matter how ugly it is. He wants it.*

Never being married or having any children before, Bruce compared being a step-dad and new husband to being a brand new student driver and getting out onto Highways 59 and 610 (the third busiest highway interchange in the nation) in Houston and being told, "Just drive, or they'll mow you over!" Immediate action is required, and it's scary! When to accelerate? When to brake? When to switch lanes? How to stay in your lane, look forward while keeping a good look in the rearview mirror! It was so much all at once! He didn't want to wreck, or for that matter, even damage the car!

I must confess, even though I am ashamed to, that I had such an attitude of harshness during the first three months of our marriage. It was really tough, those first three months, and on into the first three years. But especially the first three months. I held the thought in the back of my mind that I've already been through one divorce; I was independent, didn't need to be married and that I could do it again and survive just fine.

I want to talk to you about vows and what they mean. I think that in our society today we take them too lightly, without really understanding what it is that we are committing. We are truly making a covenant with each other as husband and wife. We are not entering into some sort of a business contract with a thirty-day notice clause! When the Lord makes a covenant with us, it is an unending promise. He is committed to us through thick and thin. In our marriage vows, we need to understand we are promising that also. My husband has been truly committed to me that way, and taught me that no matter how I behaved, he was going to love me anyway! He was never leaving. He said divorce was not a word that we were going to use in our marriage. When he explained this to me, it was as though a light bulb went off in my head. I'd always thought that divorce was a viable option. My parents were divorced, and I'd been divorced. In my mind I had strangely conjured up the thought that somehow marriage and divorce were intertwined! How crazy is that!

When you have these two thoughts so deeply inter-twined in your mind, it creates a lie. In the beginning of our marriage, I didn't have them separated and didn't have it all clear in my heart and mind.

I was emotionally fatigued, weary of working so hard to make the marriage work. I didn't feel like I had much left of me to give. I felt insecure because we'd only been married for three months! I was afraid to trust, afraid of so much. I was already taking a huge risk and wonder-ing if I'd stepped off into something that I needed to get out of.

Because of this fear, I became stubborn and selfish in the way I viewed many things. Here's another confes-sion... I felt that I was "above counseling" and was not willing to go. I was flaccid in my commitment to our marriage, because I was battling with the idea that our marriage might not work, I had thoughts of why try? I wasn't sure if I had what it was going to take to form unity in our blended family. It was overwhelming to say the least, and I wasn't sure if I was up for the challenge.

*In my mind I had strangely conjured up the thought that somehow marriage and divorce were intertwined.*

Pride kept me from being able to reach out for help and kept my heart hard. When you feel pride in this way, you need to look at it. I didn't want to hold up the mirror and really see myself. If I did, I would see my own ugliness looking back at me. That's hard to see. If you have a hard time looking at your truth, there must be a reason! It was so ugly that I refused to look at it. I encourage you to give your truth to God, no matter how ugly it is. He wants it. He wants to show you and teach you His way, His truth. He longs to give you a new heart, new eyes, and new ears to experience Him through. He is the way, the truth, and the life! Trust Him with all of your life. Oh, how He wants to give you new life, a new found freedom in His love!

Bruce had never had children, nor had he ever been married before. When we married he was thirty-one, I was twenty-seven; three days into our honeymoon was Bruce's thirty-second birthday.

Over the five months that we dated, the girls grew especially attached to Bruce. He was very good with them; they quickly grew to love him.

Marrying Bruce brought lots of change into our three lives and lots of structure that quite frankly we needed. The comical thing here is that we didn't necessarily realize we needed the change, and we weren't real keen on the structure! We certainly weren't viewing this from the perspective of it being beneficial to us! We liked the freedom of grabbing a slice of pizza and sitting down in front of the TV to eat. Yes, we did have a table, but of course that isn't what we was used it for! We used the table for homework, games, coloring, and other amusements. Very rarely for eating! I'm sure as you read this there are some of you who are grinning because you can totally relate! This is simply the way it was.

Bruce yearned for all of us to sit at the dining room table during dinner; with the TV turned *off*, and pray together prior to our meal. Throughout dinner he invited substantial and satisfying conversation. We loved our TV shows; what in the world was he trying to do to us?! I don't think he ever imagined the kind of fight he was in for with the three of us girls!

The idea of turning off the TV was absolute torture for us! We had our special shows! We had a routine! This was absolutely grueling for us. He was determined for us to buy into this idea. We were used to our routine, and liked the structure we *already* had in place. We would say, "This is the way *we* do things," trying to get *him* to conform to *us*. Little did we know that we really were the ones that were so oblivious! We were missing out on so much with one another.

> *I was letting my pride get in the way of what God needed to show me.*

He explained how he wanted to get to know us, how as we each aged and grew up, we would have new things each day to share, questions, enjoy different points of view. He wanted questions to be asked, ideas to be shared, explaining that this would enable us to always stay in touch with each other, as we grew. He insisted that this should be the way we would eat. We would always have breakfast and dinner together, no matter what.

Bruce encouraged us to look at each other with new eyes, to take new routes, to discover new paths into relationships with each other as well as with others. We, in our own ways, were doing the very same for him only in different ways.

The three of us were much more spontaneous, while he was more structured. We all believed that he needed to incorporate more fun and spontaneity into his daily living, seeing the need for him to loosen up! He needed to liven up a bit, enjoy life, breathe, relax.

Funny how Bruce brought much needed structure to our lives while we brought some much needed fun to his. It is wonderful how each of us adds a component to the other that is needed. God knows the needs of each of us and finds ways to fulfill our lives with each other. God is the balancing force that we all need.

> We don't yet see things clearly. We're squinting in a fog, peering through a mist. But it won't be long before the weather clears and the sun shines bright! We'll see it all then, see it all as clearly as God sees us, knowing him directly just as he knows us! But for right now, until that completeness, we have three things to do to lead us toward that consummation: Trust steadily in God, hope unswervingly, love extravagantly. And the best of the three is love.
>
> 1 Corinthians 13:12–13 MSG

As we continued to drive through the fog, experiencing the twists, turns and bumps in the road, sometimes it seemed as though the headlights were not able to penetrate through it. Many times it was as though I was squinting through the fog as we drove along what felt like an uncertain path. I would find myself questioning God, wondering if I would ever be able to see the light. There were a few times when I was ready to throw in the towel and be done with it and go back to the way things were before Bruce came along.

Another one of the family struggles was that the girls were jealous of my affection for Bruce. They wanted me all to themselves, and they worked hard at letting that be known. They would behave badly, and I was embarrassed by their behavior. I had raised them to be courteous and considerate of others, especially of adults. I also believe that they were testing Bruce; they wanted to see if he was really going to stay. They needed to know without a shadow of doubt that he was going to love them no matter what. In their young lives, they'd already had quite a bit of upheaval; I believe they were trying to see if he could be driven off.

> *Pride can completely annihilate what has the potential for radiance.*

They wanted to see if they could take the wheel; they wanted to see if they could be in control and split us up. It's amazing how fast pain and hurts can be poured out into behaviors of children!

Bruce is so faithful though. He is such a good man

of God. In retrospect, I am sometimes amazed that he never wanted to throw in the towel himself! We girls can be vicious! I'm not proud to say it, but it's true. We can let our loveliness leave us so fast with our ugliness that it's downright amazing! I know that many of you ladies know exactly what I'm talking about, don't you?

At other times it can also be hilarious if you have a really good sense of humor (and of course, I do, thank God!). I don't know if the men that experience it find it to be humorous, but I thank God for their patience in putting up with it!

During that really tough first three months of our marriage, Bruce suggested that we seek counseling. I was appalled by the mere suggestion of it! Me and my haughty self, boy did I have much to learn. I was letting my pride get in the way of what God really needed to show me. Pride can completely annihilate what has the potential for radiance. Pride creates such arrogance and smugness. It's a danger within us that we always need to be aware of.

> Because he is proud, that evil person doesn't turn to the Lord. There is no room for God in any of his thoughts.
>
> Psalm 10:4 NIRV

The passage above rings so true in my ears. It's hard to confess that I learned this the hard way. But I am happy to report that once learned I get it. I thank God for His Word. It reveals and teaches us so much. He wants us to know the secrets of living an abundant, joyful life with Him, if we'd only surrender to Him.

Bring it to your Lord; meditate on the Scripture

passage above and ask Him to reveal to you what you need to learn. He wants you to give him all your hurt, your pain, your fear. All the areas that you've built walls around, places that you won't let anyone in. Places where pride and arrogance are starting to root. Give it to Him so that you can stand free in His grace and love. Step out of the fog and into His light and love.

Bruce kindly and tenderly encouraged me to go to counseling with him. He knew that he would have to be gentle with me to get me to go. He found a minister, a lady in her late eighties or early nineties, by the name of Mary Katherine McDougal. He informed me that he had made the appointment and was going to go, and asked me to go, too. Here I go again! I'm ashamed to admit it, but I let my ugliness shine forth again saying, "I won't be there!" In that moment I saw for the first time Bruce's hope dissipate. I saw how I was making things worse. I was not allowing my heart or the Holy Spirit to lead me. Seeing his broken heart appear on his face is what completely melted my heart. In that instant I relinquished my ugly pride and chose to go.

When pride comes, then comes disgrace, but with humility comes wisdom.

Proverbs 11:2 NIV

> *If you are reading this and experiencing pride in your life in places that are hard for you to admit to, I'd encourage you to look it right in the eye.*

I thank God that I did. Mary Katherine was an amazing woman, and how she loved the Lord. She was much older than her husband, around thirty or forty years older! She taught us about unconditional love, tolerance, patience, staying power, fortitude, strength, courage, weakness, being devoted, and of course she helped us to find each other irresistible again!

We journeyed to her home to visit with her on a weekly basis. I looked forward to her wisdom, her prayers, and her love. She never took sides; she loved us both with parental eyes. We went for five or six weeks. It was amazing how much she educated us in such a short amount of time. She gave without expecting anything back. She never charged us for her time, but would accept what she liked to say was a "love offering." She loved "love"! She was love!

She taught us what she said were the two most important words we would ever use in our marriage: *"So what?"* She said that if we could learn *that*, we'd learn what forgiveness really means. She wanted us to utilize this in our daily thoughts when we knew that the other hadn't intentionally tried to hurt us or frustrate us. We were letting the little nit picky things that one says or does easily steal our joy. Why do we let those little things bother us so much? She taught us to say to ourselves, "So *what* if he rolls his eyes", "*So what* if she gets emotional?" It's total acceptance. Simple if we can actually do it. Acceptance creates trust, and love and value of one another. When we accept one another's true loving intentions, that is what we focus on in the other person, rather than the negative, which always brings us back to love!

> Love is patient; love is kind; love is not envious or boastful or arrogant or rude. It does not insist on its own way; it is not irritable or resentful; it does not rejoice in wrongdoing, but rejoices in the truth. It bears all things, believes all things, hopes all things, endures all things. Love never ends...
>
> 1 Corinthians 13:4–8 NRSV

We had the Scripture above read at our wedding. We thought that this passage was beautiful.

Many times we *look* at Scripture and fail to *apply* it. The Scriptures are in place for us to have life application. They are to penetrate into our minds and hearts so that we can actually begin to live them out into our lives.

In our sessions with Mary Katherine, she had us go over this passage again and learn the meaning of it. She taught us to live out forgiveness, the beauty and holiness of it. We have never been the same since! We have never looked back, never wanting to live that way again, but to live in a marriage honoring one another, and God, while fully relying upon Him. We wanted our daughters to know what a truly good marriage was, and the only way for them to know that was to witness it. We walked it, and talked it, and have lived this way since. We have been each other's best friend! These weekly sessions saved our marriage! Please do not be afraid to reach out for counseling as a couple; your marriage and family are worth it.

We have modeled for our kids what a truly happy, solid marriage is. They now know what to look for in their partners.

Bruce and I are so blessed today. Before Bruce marries couples, we have the couples over to our home to visit with them, get to know them, pray for them, encourage them, and mentor them. We've come to realize that the couples need his perspective as a husband, as well as my perspective as a wife. Over the several visits with those who are engaged, one of the things we insert is the very important message of "So What!" and everything else that Mary Katherine taught us! We love reminding them of the marriage beyond just the wedding day. It's a process that we find to be a precious time with them. There are so many details to plan for the wedding itself, we don't want them to forget about their life ahead. It's such a sweet time for me to be able to share with them. Reminding them how to hold their marriage in high regard, to understand the vows that they are taking, and to live into them with gusto and with joy!

Being in ministry affords us the opportunity to be *inserted* into the lives of so many! While doing so, we *insert* the wisdom that has been passed on to us from others who walk with God in their lives! All the folks that the Lord has placed in our lives have brought us such richness. They have been what I like to call "Holy Spirit Connectors." This is the part of ministry we love!

And to think that I almost threw in the towel, and didn't learn to drive! I would have missed so many wonderful things along the way. I must say that I'm a pretty good driver.

Remember as you drive along this road of life, as you journey onward be sure to keep the headlights on, especially on those dark nights. Look for all of the signs along the way to keep you on the right path. Pray that the Lord will be your driver, illuminating your way, and when you begin to veer off course that His light will bring you back on track.

> *Many times we look at Scripture and fail to apply it. The Scriptures are in place for us to have life application. They are to penetrate into our minds and hearts so that we can actually begin to live them.*

Make an effort not to talk so much that you miss out on what He and others have to say while on the drive.

Always be open to the open road! Drive! Take pleasure in the journey! Stop along the way to not only smell the roses, but gather them. See the roses in the people you meet, soak in the *Son!* Never ever forget the value of saying *"So What!?"*

## Life's Fancy Road

Along this fancy road of life
Take time to smell the flowers
Lest we become jaded and trite
Amid congested hours—

The road is long and sometimes worn
As we attempt to find,
Elusive roses amongst the thorns
Evading grasping minds.

The distant rhythmic music of life
Pulsating through the fog
Lends reason to pause—examine the skies
Take notice of what we log.

This ever changing highway stretches
Amongst the hidden streams
Becoming smooth–then filled with patches
Life seems a chameleon.

It is of interest for us to note
However winding the road
When least expected and too remote
Spring bursts forth from cold!

Then let us travel with joyful account
And know on this fancy road
The beauty perceived is all about
It's how we envision our load!

A poem written by my mother,
Doris Ann Gash Rich, 1984.

# CALLING IT QUITS...

*Bruce leaves his career to pursue his calling*

Every good and perfect gift is from above, coming down from the Father of the heavenly lights, who does not change like shifting shadows.

James 1:17 NIV

> *Our lives were changing before us,*
> *but God never changes.*

Our lives were changing before us, but God never changes.

Before Bruce and I married, he'd let me know of His calling to become a priest in the Episcopal Church. I expressed to him that I'd felt a call to ministry as well, and wasn't quite sure what it looked like.

While we were dating and during the first four years of our marriage, Bruce was a civilian working at Bergstrom Air Force Base in Southeast Austin. During the week his job was working as a civilian, and one weekend a month he was a reservist in the 924th Tactical Fighter Group. In the evenings he was going to school finishing up his degree. This went on for several years. He needed to get his degree in order to go to seminary. At this time we had no idea that the base would be closing.

As the years went by, Bruce was getting close to acquiring his degree, and we had begun the process of preparing for seminary, which included the process of becoming a postulant for Holy Orders in the Episcopal Church in the Diocese of Texas. When you are a postulant, you are guaranteed placement in a church upon completion of seminary. Each year they only accept two or three postulants. We'd written our autobiographical summaries, and we'd both interviewed with the bishop, gone through all of the interviews with several discernment committees, the Standing Committee, and the Commission on Ministry. It was a lengthy process, and we actually enjoyed it! I know that many don't enjoy that process but we really did. We were blessed to be one of the few to be granted postulancy. We praise God for that. This was a huge hurdle that carried us through some difficult times during those seminary years. It was truly the provision of our amazing God. We are humbled by it and so thankful.

> *Isn't it funny that we can have relationship with things and become emotionally attached to them?*

When George H.W. Bush was in office, the administration began making plans for military base closures. Bill Clinton became President in 1993, and his administration continued carrying out the plans of military base closures. They had plans to close or consolidate 105 military bases (Weiner, Tim. "Decrying Base-Closing Plan as an 'Outrage,' the President Gives a Grudging Go-Ahead". *The New York Times,* July 14, 1995.). In 1991 there were plans for approximately 26 closures, in 1993 approximately 28 and in 1995, approximately 27 closures (www.globalsecurity.org).

The Lord was guiding us through it all as we continued to trust Him for His wisdom, guidance, and provision during the postulancy process. Bruce had finished up with school and now was degreed.

As we went along with the process of entering seminary, Bruce was going to have to leave his civilian job. As the Lord would have it, the base was now offering the opportunity to volunteer to leave early and receive full retirement benefits. Bruce was leaving with fifteen years in, but with the closure, he was able to leave with the retirement package of twenty years in. What a blessing that would be for us when he became eligible to receive those benefits! Bruce left his civilian job and started seminary in 1992. He continued to serve as a reservist until 1995, which provided a small amount of income for us. We also had some of funds from the GI bill for his education.

During the last few years of college before entering into seminary, we were in a preparatory mode, wanting to pay off bills, and become debt free. Part of that process was scaling down our vehicles, getting away from expensive car payments. We both had vehicles that we loved! Isn't it funny that we can have relationship with things, and become emotionally attached to them? Bruce drove a Ford Bronco II, and it was such a fun ride! It was in perfect condition, and it also was what he'd driven while he was single. Bruce and I had a sentimental attachment to it. We went on our first date in the Bronco. We had driven all the way to Missouri in that Bronco. His first proposal was in that Bronco. We planned our entire wedding in that Bronco. We'd taken various family trips to the zoo, Schlitterbahn, Aquarena Springs, Wonder Caves and Inner Space Caverns in that Bronco. The memories in that Bronco are endless!

I was driving the most wonderful Toyota Previa. It was the most incredible mini-van of it's time! Oh, I loved it! The girls were so active in school and had so many friends. We had outings with the youth group and took major road trips in it. All of their friends loved it because it had two electric slide windows in the roof. They loved to stand up and wave out the windows and pretend that they were movie stars waving to their adoring fans! The girls were involved in musicals and plays and gymnastics, cheerleading and choir. The room for changing clothes in the back seats was great. When we went on major road trips, the girls could have there very own seats. Talk about a sanity saver for us! We loved it!

Bruce sold his wonderful Bronco and paid cash for a teeny tiny little Ford Festiva, which we affectionately called his "seminary roller skate." It did the job, though. I sold my wonderful van and paid cash for a used white Ford Taurus. It was in good condition, and it got us where we needed to go. This was our primary means of transportation as a family. If we had friends come along with the girls, it was pretty cozy. We were so thankful not to have car payments, though!

In the late 1980s and in to the early 90s it was a really difficult time, and the economy was in a major recession. Homeowners and business were defaulting on their loans and going through foreclosure. Jobs were scarce; people were getting laid off and couldn't keep up with payments. They began to literally walk away from their homes. Houston was becoming a ghost town. I was in property management at the time in the Austin area; we were doing everything we could to lease apartments. We just wanted warm bodies in there to occupy them! There were so many new homes and new apartment communities, and commercial buildings that had been built, and they were all sitting vacant!

Things began to turn around in the early to mid 1990s. In 1991 we purchased our home. It had been a foreclosure. It had been a model home; therefore it had all of the upgrades, sprinkler system, higher grade carpet, and incredible drapes throughout. It was beautiful! We placed our bid on it and won the bid! We'd placed a previous bid on the very same floor plan in the same neighborhood and didn't get it. We felt like God was saving this house for us. We were grateful to have won the bid. It afforded us a very low monthly payment.

When we were entering seminary in 1993, the economy was going strong, and rental rates were on the rise. Jobs were being filled, companies were doing well. People were feeling secure again.

We considered selling the house and moving into an apartment to save even more money. As we began to explore that option, we realized that a two bedroom apartment was more expensive than our three bedroom house. The economy was recovering nicely and in view of that fact, we were able to stay in our home. Being able to continue to reside in our home brought much relief to me as a woman needing to nest and have some sort of stability.

> *He experienced the love of our Lord in various ways, through family and friends. He also had some profound and wonderful experiences with angels.*

In the midst of all this we'd been given a devastating blow. Bob, Bruce's dad, had been diagnosed with cancer, a brain tumor. Oh, how we grieved this news. His parents, Bob and Donna, were living in Mont Clair, New Jersey. Bob had also been an Episcopal priest for many years. He was Stewardship Director for the National Episcopal Church. In light of the diagnosis, they chose to move back home to be closer to family, friends and MD Anderson Hospital.

The news was so unexpected. Our hearts were aching. I will never forget this pain. It was so odd for us to think that he could be leaving us. Bruce and I had only been married for such a short time. We were afraid, and yet hopeful, because Bob was always in such good health and he was so young.

Bob and Donna began the journey of doctor visits and diagnosis. He had a rather aggressive tumor and during a short amount of time had two major brain surgeries. It was rough on him. Due to the surgery, he lost part of his eyesight; he could still see but explained that it was sort of like seeing through mini-blinds.

He experienced the love of our Lord in various ways, through family and friends. He also had some profound and wonderful experiences with angels. He was able to experience their beauty and actually communicate with them in the hospital and in their living room at home. He shared these stories with us and I have never forgotten them. He always said that he wanted to see *real* angels and he did! I have encouraged Donna to write about them, as I believe they are miraculous moments that they had. I know that we all have the desire to communicate with heavenly angels. We want to know more about the Holy Spirit world. In the wonderful moments that Bob told me of his angel encounters, I felt like I had a special connection to them all my own because of the emotion he had in sharing with me. I know more about them than I ever did before. I experience love and grace in a more meaningful way because of what he shared with me about the angels. I saw the tears filled with awestruck tenderness when he spoke of them. I felt a certain amount of what he felt as he shared his amazing experiences with me. I'm forever grateful that he was able to give me the glimpse.

Bruce's parents, Bob and Donna, were such a special gift in my life. Of course, Donna still is. She and I are close. Both Bob and Donna loved me and the girls. They welcomed us with open arms into the family. It felt so good. I was able to connect with both of them on a deep spiritual level. It was very gratifying and comforting to me. I love them so much. They taught me about unconditional love, love freely given with no strings attached, complete acceptance! Just like Christ. At this point Bruce and I had been married for four years. I didn't feel like I had Bob in my life long enough. He was so fun, so spontaneous!

> *They taught me about unconditional love, love freely given with no strings attached, complete acceptance! Just like Christ.*

After the two surgeries it became apparent that the cancer wasn't going away. They tried to remove it all, but it wasn't possible. It began to grow again and rapidly at that. Bob tried to go through chemo and he couldn't do it; it was too hard on him. In 1993, just after Bruce entered into seminary, Bob went home to be with our Lord. Bruce and I miss him dearly. So do the girls.

Be merciful to me, O Lord, for I am in distress; my eyes grow weak with sorrow, my soul and my body with grief.

Psalm 31:9 NIV

✕

I was working back in property management, and previous to that I'd been able to take off for about a year to enjoy the girls and be home with them more. I savored this time! The girls were able to get involved with acting a bit and were in live performances in the Georgetown Palace Theatre. With that came all of the rehearsals to go to. They were in *The Jungle Book*. Kellie Ann had a part of one of the little girls, and Tabitha had the part of a talking and singing buzzard! Oh the good ol' days!

As Bruce began seminary, I was burdened with the financial pressures for our family. Working countless days of overtime, even into the nights I worked. I suffered the intense economic saddle, and it was weighty much of the time.

After enjoying being a stay-at-home mom, I had to force myself to go back to work and carry the financial load over the next several years during seminary. I worked long, hard hours, and I honestly do have some regrets about the hours put in. I always tell young mothers that if I could turn back the hands of time, the one thing I would change would have been to be a stay-at-home mom. If it's at all possible, stay home with the kids; have fun in all there is to being a mommy! It's such a wonderful time, and it goes by so quickly! Oh, how I missed spending the time with the girls and with Bruce.

I worked for some really great management companies. I was in leadership roles within the organizations. It was there that I learned so much about leadership. I know that this has been a wonderful part of my journey, part of the process of becoming who the Lord has created me to be.

Each person put in our path, whether pleasant or unpleasant, teaches us, coaches us, and edifies us. They grow us in our faith. We learn what to do and what *not* to do in business and personal living.

I thank God for the people in my life who were full of integrity; I looked up to them and allowed them to mentor me along the way. I learned how to operate a team with integrity and grow them and myself into people who function out of love, rather than other means.

Love and truth form a good leader; sound leadership
is founded on loving integrity.

Proverbs 20:28 MSG

---

*Each person put in our path, whether pleasant or unpleasant, teaches us, coaches us, and edifies us. They grow us in our faith. We learn what to do and what not to do in business and personal living.*

---

I continually desire for learning to rely on my Lord for all my needs; praying to Him for the guidance as a wife and a mother is part of my journey. Delving into His word, asking Him to shape me, and to remake me into what he'd have me be, this process continues; it is never finished. As we grow older, we realize how little we know. I yearn to continue to grow in and with Christ always. I remain awed and amazed at all He has for me to learn from His written word.

> Good leadership is a channel of water controlled by God; He directs it to whatever ends He chooses.
>
> Proverbs 21:1 MSG

Men have a need to provide for and take care of their families. I think that Bruce, as a man longing to be the provider for his family, found it difficult for me to be the sole provider. He was very proactive about us paying down all of our debt and purchasing good reliable transportation without having any kind of monthly payments attached. He was truly leading our house properly and was taking all the measures possible for the financial burdens to be as light as possible. He listened to what God was showing him, and took every precaution for our family.

My mother in law provided for our house payment the entire time of our years in seminary. She is always fair to all of her kids, and she let us know that it would be deducted from our inheritance. Bruce and I were so grateful for her gift to us then. It was a comfort in the midst of much discomfort. And yet with the way the Lord was providing, we did have a peace in the midst of our stress. There are many times when you are in the heart of God's calling, it can be hard, and treacherous; yet in the midst of all of it you experience a peace that truly is beyond all understanding. God gives you His peace as you journey up the hill.

Bruce knew that this journey we were traveling on wasn't going to be a smooth one. He had once watched a documentary about St. Francis of Assisi. St. Francis and his monks were traveling through some villages and came to a fork in the road. In one direction the path was smooth, downhill, and would be easily traveled. In the other direction the path was arduous, rocky, steep, and laborious. They asked St. Francis which road to take, and he said the difficult path.

That knowing remained with Bruce as we began the journey through seminary. Largely due to the fact that Bruce has dyslexia, he knew this would be the path that he was going to have to take.

---

*As we grow older, we realize how little we know.*

---

Dyslexia has been trying for Bruce over the years, but I have to say that it has also been a gift. It has caused me to see a brilliant man in him. He is one who never quits, never gives up! It has caused him to have an inner strength that I've not seen in most folks. Bruce is visionary and sees further down the road than most. He is patient and persevering; he's willing to sweat, to climb the steep hill and head toward the goal that Christ is calling him to. Even when others doubt it can be done, not Bruce! He is faithful to his call; he is obedient to God even if it isn't easy. He is a good man, and I've learned so much from him. I am proud to be his wife and proud to be in ministry with him.

I think that so many times people think that if God has called them to something, then all the doors should swing wide open for them, thinking everything should fall right into place, no obstacles should they have to climb. It should be easy street. If not, then they are quick to let it go and say something like, "Oh well, I guess it wasn't meant to be; otherwise we wouldn't have any of this struggle. God would just remove all the obstacles in order for us to go for it."

Let me just say this: if God has called you, He has called you. Bottom line. When He calls you to something, He doesn't always make it easy. Many times He does test you. He is committed to *transforming* you along the way. He is going to grow you, stretch you, and prune you in areas that you need the pruning. He's going to humble you, cause you to surrender to Him by getting on your knees before Him and have you proclaim to Him Lord, Lord, have it Your way, not mine! He's going to work on your pride, your ego. He's going to make sure that you learn to recognize His voice (not a voice that sounds sort of like His). He wants to begin a new work in you. If you are going to be an ambassador for Him, He wants you to represent Him well. Any of us who think we can do that all on our own, think again!

If you are committed to Him, be committed to the process that He has in store for you. Trust that He only has the best intentions for you. This I know to be true; this I don't question, ever! He is the Creator of the world, He is the Creator of all. You and I must learn to truly bow down before Him and give Him the honor and glory that He fully deserves!

I also feel the need to say something more. You don't have to be ordained to be chosen by God to be a servant for Him. Each of us is hand-picked with a purpose. Hand-picked by the Holy Lord! Enjoy the journey, even the struggle. We can remain joyful in the struggle, because the joy of the Lord really does live in us, as it is one of the fruits of the Spirit! Because it is one of the fruits of the Spirit, He can and does give you joy in the midst of the struggle. He can give you joy and peace, and it is His good pleasure to do so.

All praise to the King! Praise Him in your journey, lift your hands in praise, sing a new song unto Him! Rejoice that He has chosen you to be His servant! There is no greater honor!

# THE SEMINARY YEARS, ABSOLUTE DROUGHT

*Our undercurrent always the breath of God blowing through our hearts, minds and bodies.*

By the end of our seminary years, we'd experienced such lack and such abundance all at the same time. In our season of drought, we became familiar with our own weakness and God's strength. We knew weak arms, legs shaking, nose running, tongue parched, voices dry and brittle, not much more than a whisper, no energy. Bruce and I relied on each other in our weakest moments. Bruce needing me; me needing Bruce; each of us needing the other to bring the other a much needed drink of reassurance; both of us in prayer. I remained in a constant state of prayer, praying that I would have the strength when he was weakest, and that he would have the strength when I was weakest. Side by side we continue to go... believing, expecting, requesting, hoping, trusting... Our undercurrent always the breath of God blowing through our hearts, minds and bodies.

> But blessed is the man who trusts me, God, the woman who sticks with God. They're like trees replanted in Eden, putting down roots near the rivers—Never a worry through the hottest of summers, never dropping a leaf, Serene and calm through droughts, bearing fresh fruit every season.
>
> Jeremiah 17:7 MSG

I can honestly say that I have never not trusted God. Yes, of course, I've questioned Him, been angry with Him, cried out to Him, wondered what He was doing and why. In those moments I always knew He was up to something, knew He was teaching me and He wanted me to learn the lesson, learn to recognize His voice as teacher. In the most difficult times of my life, I've never let go of my trust in God. I hang onto that with everything that I am. I hear Him. I know Him. I know that His plan for me is perfect. I really do believe that. I have no doubt here. His word tells me that he has a plan for me and that it's not to harm me. I know this to be true. If you are currently going through what seems a drought, trust me, I know what that is. I also know that it is for good; it is to grow you closer to Him, to weave you into Him. Let your ego go, and allow Him to be the biggest part of you. Lay down the things that are not genuine, not valid, and not suitable. Pick up those things of honor, things of real value, so that you glorify Him and reap the rewards. In so doing you honor yourself, and most importantly you honor God, bringing you peace, and joy and good sleep.

I am Lady Wisdom, and I live next to Sanity; Knowledge and Discretion live just down the street. The Fear-of-God means hating Evil, whose ways I hate with a passion—pride and arrogance and crooked talk. Good counsel and common sense are my characteristics; I am both Insight and the Virtue to live it out. With my help, leaders rule, and law-makers legislate fairly; With my help, governors govern, along with all in legitimate authority. I love those who love me; those who look for me find me. Wealth and Glory accompany me—also substantial Honor and a Good Name. My benefits are worth more than a big salary, even a very big salary; the re-turns on me exceed any imaginable bonus. You can find me on Righteous Road—that's where I walk— at the intersection of Justice Avenue, Handing out life to those who love me, filling their arms with life—armloads of life!

Proverbs 8:12 MSG

> *Many times I've had thoughts that God has a way of appearing rude*

I, Wisdom, live together with good judgment. I know where to discover knowledge and discernment.

Proverbs 8:12 NLT

Many times I've had thoughts that God has a way of

appearing rude, but I know that isn't true. He has a way of bringing you closer to Him that can feel so lonely. He has a way of dehydrating you, so that you are completely parched. Have you ever found yourself questioning His motive? Questioning His love? Questioning His purpose, His calling for you, the purpose and calling that you know you heard clearly? Still believing in the purpose and the calling, still knowing that you weren't wrong about it, yet somehow questioning Him and the way He brings you to Himself. Finding yourself in a debate with Him, asking what He's doing, and why He's doing it in such a way that makes you feel so far away from Him. Causing you to become completely parched and exhausted, with cracked lips, thirsty for water in the wilderness.

We have been conditioned to believe that if we are in His will all the doors should fly open, that it should be easy breezy. We have somehow conjured up this crazy expectation that if God wants us to do something, if He is calling us to be His servants, it should be so easy. No obstacles to overcome, no hurdles to jump. No doors will be shut. If it's not easy or takes any kind hard work, or if a door appears to be shutting, then that's it, we quit, we must not have heard Him right. We shouldn't have to work this hard for anything if God called us to it. We give up too easily these days. We somehow believe that we shouldn't have to struggle if we are doing the very thing that the Lord has called us to.

I have actually heard people say things like, "I don't believe that if God called me to this that it would be this hard." If He had really wanted me to do it, He would have made it easy."

I will concur that many times that is the case. However, many times it is not. When the Lord calls you to Him and you hear Him calling, don't expect it to be easy; don't expect it to be hard. Expect it to be His will for you, whatever that looks like. Accept what's in front of you and the challenge of it. How wonderful the challenge is! (Remember that I said *challenge,* which means that it's not easy; otherwise it would not be a challenge.) I have had both things happen. I have had the struggle in His call, and I have had the easy breeziness of His call. I have learned that they both create powerful change in your life.

> *To believe in His perfect plan, to walk into the scary places with a faith so big, or with a faith so small, that I experience faith to the fullest. So that I know what faith is.*

They both co-exist in this world together. Our Lord has a wonderful way of bringing balance to us. As I reflect back on the way that He has moved in my life, I wouldn't change the dry places for anything! I have grown to appreciate the questioning that happens there. I have learned to love my total reliance upon Him. I have learned to ask Him the hard questions, to hear what He has to say, to experience what He has to show me, who He wants me to be, how He wants me to be. He wants me to be His! To believe in His perfect plan, to walk into the scary places with a faith so big, or with a faith so small, that I experience faith to the fullest, so that I know what faith is. Faith is so amazing, people! If you hear anything as you read this, hear what it is that I am trying to tell you about faith. You find it in the most interesting ways. You find faith in the small cracks of a person's smile that you don't even know. I found faith one day while driving down the road; the person in the vehicle in front of me had a bumper sticker that simply had the words FAITH! It was a black bumper sticker with big bold capital letters that simply said FAITH! I had just submitted several book proposals in the mail for this book series and had just checked my mailbox. In the mailbox was a letter of acceptance and a contract from the publishing house! I followed the car down the road a bit with tear-filled eyes fixed on the word FAITH! I was brought to the realization that I, along with you, am on a journey of faith as I followed the car with the bumper sticker on it. This is one of the ways our God speaks to us! He places the things in front of us that cause us to think on Him, to believe Him! He knows our needs. He knows what's going to grab hold of us, grab hold of our hearts! He loves grabbing hold of our hearts, and He loves it when we follow Him!

You begin to realize so much more when you realize that this life is full of purpose, full of promise, full of love, full of hurt, full of need, full of you, full of human beings who want it. Find your faith; look for it in the hardest of times, and in the most glorious of times. Love your faith. Never lose your faith. Go ahead and question it, because when you do, that's when you grow, that's when you will know; then you will be shown the answers to your questions. Then you are in connection and in relationship with the Lord God! Wow! What an amazing journey He has each of us on! I want for you to WANT God with everything you are! If you are frustrated with where you are with God right now, that is GREAT! Keep wrestling with it! Commit to that, commit to finding Him. He is in relationship with you during these times, usually more profoundly than any other times of your life.

I know that commitment to His calling is first. Commitment is such a difficult thing these days on our microwave society. If we would shift the perspective to "commitment is lovely" rather than "commitment is hard", we would recognize the beauty and strength in it. The result? Trust. Then trust is not questioned, it simply is. It would not be broken.

---

*Find your faith; look for it in the hardest of times, and in the most glorious of times. Love your faith. Never lose your faith. Go ahead and question it, because when you do, that's when you grow.*

---

Many times in society today, if marriage becomes hard, or work, or a struggle, we are so quick to give up! The labor, the work that you put into it is what makes you appreciate it so much more. With Christ, with your spouse, you become bonded as you co-labor together. You create a masterpiece of His reflection. You are able to stand back and look at what He's had you build. Yes, you remember the days of sweat and tears. Yes, you remember the days of child rearing. Yes, you remember the financial stresses. Yes, you remember the days of going through family illness, death, holidays, birthdays! Yes, you remember the days of ice cold tea, and cool breezes, and music flowing through the living room as you dance; the carving of pumpkins! All of it! It all builds the foundation of trust.

Earlier in my statement when I said that God has a way of appearing rude, I said that because I want you to know that He is the exact opposite. He is not rude. He can bring you to a place of extreme. A place that feels so harsh, so empty. But in those places it is where you truly find Him, when you can not rely upon yourself any longer. He wants you to become humble, to become reliant upon His strength, His mercy, His grace, His love, His provision, His wisdom, His passion, His laughter, His glory, His nature, His power. He wants you to live into your calling, so that it is ALL about Him. Until He gets you to that place, you will never truly be living out your calling. He has such a vision for you. He has such a trust in you! He believes in you, He places His trust in YOU! He needs to get you to a place where you put all of your trust in Him! This is huge! This is what it's all about. You must be taken through the experiences of "Where are you God" in order to find Him! My experience has been that when we feel as though God has left us, He is actually closer to us than He has ever been before. Remember this: when you feel like He is absent, He is closer to you than He has ever been. Never forget that. He is bringing you to a place of growth, spiritually maturing you, even if you are not asking for it! How rude! Ha! How rude that He wants to bring us to Him even if we don't want Him to! How rude that He wants to be in relationship with you! How rude that He wants you to want that, too! Oh no, my friends, it's not rude at all; it's lovely, it's beautiful, it's grace, it's precious love, given to you and to me from the Lord of Lords, the King of Kings, the Creator and Sustainer of the Universe!

## Our First Seminary Gathering

> *If you choose to do life without God, what course would you be on right now?*

In the first year of seminary, we were in the stage of romanticizing ministry. I think that everyone who thinks about ministry thinks about all the wonderful things that come with it. We don't realistically look at the way the world is. We are in a state of bliss, the honeymoon stage of seminary. This stage wasn't meant to last too long for us...

We were so excited to be attending our very first gathering in the chapel at the seminary, along with all of the other seminarians and spouses! We felt honored as we walked up the sidewalk toward the chapel! There were enormous oak trees with years of wisdom, and long graceful arms inviting us in. We were awed by the beauty of this place, and the years of promise ahead of us. We were going to be among an apostolic tradition of men to receive Holy Orders. We were struck with sentiment, and the beauty of the chapel and the years of tradition. We all entered, and mingled, and visited, meeting new people from around the country, all who had been called by God.

Taking our seats, and partaking in prayer, standing and singing ancient hymns, we were in a state of bliss. One of the professors who was also ordained stepped into the pulpit and began to address each of us with greetings and welcomes. Then we all gasped in the most silent of gasps, which pronounced it even further for me as we sat shocked at what we heard! We were told that if we expected to find a spiritual community here, we were sadly mistaken! Heads turned, mouths a bit ajar; eyes with question marks could be seen on most of the faces. In that moment we clung to our romantic belief, not wanting to believe what we'd just heard.

> God grabbed me. God's Spirit took me up and set me down in the middle of an open plain strewn with bones. He led me around and among them—a lot of bones! There were bones all over the plain—dry bones, bleached by the sun.
>
> Ezekiel 37:1–2 MSG

It's amazing how in the moment when we are told something that doesn't resonate with *our* vision, *our* plan that we begin to question the plan, question God. In my learning and in my getting to know God, it's in these moments that we know that God is moving, teaching, and growing us in our faith and spiritual maturity. Start asking Him the questions; ask Him, *what do you want me to get from this?* Looking back on this I now know that what the seminary professors wanted for us. They wanted us to have our strength in Christ, not in them, or in man. In the midst of it we were angered by their seeming lack of care, which kept us from hearing God.

After "doing" seminary for a while, the reality hit of how much work it was. How much pressure Bruce was carrying was beginning to show. So many different burdens to bear! We had more than one kind of struggle. There were our two young daughters, financial burdens, time constraints because of all the reading and homework to be done. Bruce is dyslexic, and that is where the challenge became extreme. Yet in the same breath, I can say it is what gave us deepened desire and strength. It caused us to examine our character, as well as our calling.

> *Whose voice is getting in the way*
> *of your joy?*

We, in our calling, began to ask the question, "Do we want this call?"..."Is it worth it?" Saying to each other it would be a lot easier to give it up, go back to what we know. Go back to what's easier. Drop it all, leave it all behind, turn and walk away. Yep, we could go on down the road and "never look back." Where we got stuck was that we realized the big lie; we would always look back, and we would always have regret. We would always wonder, we would walk away with broken hearts, we would have said no to God. We could not choose to say no. We could not live with that kind of regret. We yearned to heed the call. We fervently wanted to stay the course! We want all that comes with the hard road! We will experience the rough ground ahead, a few skinned knees and broken fingernails, as well as bruised egos at times. It's okay, we'll take it. We choose it! Yes, we choose you, Lord, we go, we go together following you, trusting you, listening to you, worshipping you. If we were to give up, I don't think we would have been truly called. I don't think that if you are truly called, you are capable of giving it up. I honestly don't think it's possible. I personally don't think that you can turn away from a call like this. I know that the struggle can cause you to have doubt, and raise many questions. I encourage you to ask these questions of yourself: Do you remember what your passion feels like? If there was only one thing you could do in your life, what would that be? What are you afraid of? Whose voice is getting in the way of your joy? This is how you get to know God and what He has in store for you. This is where you get to know more of yourself, too. You get to find out what you're made of, how you're wired. You get to find out what passion is; you get to find out if your passion is scary. You get to find out how you face your fears. You get to choose to be driven by your faith or your fear. We always stand in choice; *God made us free to choose.* We have so many choices to make in any one given day. How are you making choices? Do you realize that the way you handle one choice can change your entire life? Do you choose to walk with God or without Him?

Take a look at this one choice positioned here before you and how the answer to this one question, according to what you choose, can change your entire life. If you choose to do life without God, what course would you be on right now? If you choose to do life with God, would be different for you?

The first day sitting in the seminary chapel, we were not really aware of the choice we were given that day. We didn't even realize that we were actually in a place of choice at the time. We were, in fact, being given the choice to rely on others or to rely on God. It was a journey of many journeys ahead. We continue on today. We have been able to find the newness of life in the journey. The living water along the way gives us the ability to dance, run, sing, praise, worship, adore, give love, receive love, know God, let God be known. Operate with tears of joy and fall on bended knee, not out of exhaustion but out of adoration!

He said to me, "Son of man, can these bones live?" I said, "Master God, only you know that." He said to me, "Prophesy over these bones: 'Dry bones, listen to the Message of God!'" God, the Master, told the dry bones, "Watch this: I'm bringing the breath of life to you and you'll come to life. I'll attach ligaments to you, put meat on your bones, cover you with skin, and breathe life into you. You'll come alive and you'll realize that I am God!" I prophesied just as I'd been commanded. As I prophesied, there was a sound and, oh, rustling! The bones moved and came together, bone to bone. I kept watching. Ligaments formed, then muscles on the bones, then skin stretched over them. But they had no breath in them. He said to me, "Prophesy to the breath. Prophesy, son of man. Tell the breath, 'God, the Master, says, Come from the four winds. Come, breath. Breathe on these slain bodies. Breathe life!'" So I prophesied, just as he commanded me. The breath entered them and they came alive! They stood up on their feet, a huge army.

Ezekiel 37: 3–10 MSG

*You get to choose to be driven by your faith or your fear. We always stand in choice, God made us free to choose. We have so many choices to make in any one given day. How are you making choices? Do you realize that the way you handle one choice can change your entire life? Do you choose to walk with God or without Him?*

In our choosing to walk with Him into His will for us, He breathes life into us, empowers us, and makes us come alive!! In the midst of learning to conform to His great will and great call upon our lives, we trust in our Lord to lead us to a holy place with Him. To places we never have imagined. To breathe life into us in such ways that we could never fathom! I am here to tell you that God has a way of bringing you closer to Him in ways that only work for you. The way He brings me to Himself will be totally different from the ways He brings you to Himself; yet we share in some similarities.

Choosing to follow your calling requires many sacrifices for you and your family, and yet the rewards are incredible! We knew we were embarking on an entirely new walk of faith. When the Lord calls you into ministry, He doesn't promise that you won't have to give things up, but He does promise His presence the entire way through. You will experience beauty with new eyes, new ways of hearing, with a new heart. You will see beauty in things that you would never have called beautiful before.

> And now, God, do it again—bring rains to our drought-stricken lives, So those who planted their crops in despair will shout hurrahs at the harvest, So those who went off with heavy hearts will come home laughing, with armloads of blessing.
>
> Psalm 126:4 MSG

# HOW DID PAULA KNOW?

> *You will see beauty in things that you would never have called beautiful before.*

I was truly afraid of Paula. I had seen her curse out the priest with a vengeance! I wanted no part of her! When Paula called and said she was coming over, I thought that *I* was going to minister to *her!*

God has a funny way of placing people in your life. I'm sure that there have been times when people have surfaced in your life for one reason or another that you did not want there. There is a particular woman who surfaced in my life that I didn't always want there. I didn't like her hardness. Her viewpoint on life was very different from mine. We were complete opposites in our thinking. Yet, both of us were deep thinkers; both of us held deep convictions within our very souls. Both of us took God very seriously and yet very differently. She was brought into my life to strengthen my faith at a time when my faith was faltering. She was the only one who saw that my faith was faltering because she knew exactly what it was to have faltering faith! When my dearest friends didn't see it, she did. She knew life on a different level than I. She brought life to me on a different level. She expanded my mind, and I became one of compassion for her. It is amazing this life! When I finally made the choice to allow her into my life, I believe God used her to strengthen my faith at a time when I needed it.

Paula was unexpectedly brought into my life! I was not looking for her to be my friend; in fact I didn't want her to be my friend; I honestly didn't like her! She kept showing up in my life, and quite frankly, I really tried to avoid her. God would not allow me to. He had other plans!

It was at church that we met. Paula had a look about her that scared me. She was tough and cussed like a sailor! She wore her feelings intensely on her face! When Paula felt something, you knew about it, and so did everyone else! She had an extremely expressive face. Paula expressed her thoughts and opinions, and felt all of her emotions loudly. When she was angry, she had a scowl, the most incredible frown one could imagine. The opposite was also true when she felt joy and was laughing; she could be heard just as loudly when she thought something was humorous. When she laughed, she was exuberant, and hooted hard and loud!

I had signed up for a class at church, and she signed up also. Both of us showed up for the class, and I honestly thought about saying I just came up to the church to adjust the bulletin board in order not to be there with her! Paula just rubbed me the wrong way. After having that awful thought, I distinctly remember shooting up one of those real quick "arrow prayers" straight up to God, saying, "God, please help me to deal with her in the upcoming weeks of this class!" I also remember saying to Him, "Lord, why do you keep having her around me?" I wasn't saying these prayers in a loving way, if you know what I mean! They were said in frustration! Have you ever prayed or spoken to God that way? I'm sure that you can relate to this. Think about those who have come into your life that you don't feel you really want there. Then begin to visit with God about them. Before you completely shut a person out of your life, realize that God has most likely placed him or her there for a reason. From my experience, He always knows what He's doing. It's always for our good, our spiritual growth and for us to see Him in them.

> *When I finally made the choice to allow her into my life, I believe God used her to strengthen my faith at a time when I needed it!*

During one of the classes the pastor said something that seemed to raise a concern with her. She began to question him, asking him to further explain. When he tried, she became incensed and began to take her fists and *beat* her thighs. Then very loudly, she began to shout, "No, no, no, no, no!" It was a startling moment for me as well as the pastor. One thing you must know, though, she was very serious about God. She truly loved the Lord. I could see the rage in her about to explode. She began to have tears stream down her face. No one in the room knew what had upset her so. No one knew what to do at that moment. I began to feel the need to reach out to her quickly!

She grabbed her son and stormed out of the church! They got into her car and squealed out of the parking lot! None of us was sure what had just happened in there. We didn't know if she would be back ever again. (I secretly hoped that she wouldn't be back and wondered if the pastor felt the same way.)

I had to remind myself that He developed her personality, and He knit her together in her mother's womb.

The following Sunday she was back. She continued to take the class. She didn't have any more of those kinds of outbursts. However, it became very apparent that she was finding her way. She was in love with our Lord! She had a deeply rooted conviction. Her passion for Him began to speak silently, yet clearly, to me. I still remained cautious with her, not letting her get too close to me. The class ended, and I would see her each Sunday at church and continued to keep my distance.

Paula was a single mom. She had one son, whom she loved fiercely. She literally lived from paycheck to paycheck.

Several months went by. I always planned the ladies retreats along with some other wonderful ladies in the church. We held the retreats every six months. I loved planning and preparing these retreats! The women of the church were (and are to this day) extraordinary. They were deep, they were fun, they laughed, and they were the deepest of friends. We all shared the common bond in that we all loved the Lord. We all drew closer to one another and to our Lord at each retreat.

At each retreat we always had a prayer partner. Normally when I was going to match up prayer partners, I would pray that the Lord would guide me in the process of pairing each of the partners. He always guided me. I would look at each name and ask the Lord who I should pair up, and I would select the prayer partner's name.

> *Before you completely shut a person out of your life, realize that God has most likely placed him or her there for a reason.*

This time I decided to pair everyone up a little differently. The idea came to me to have different colors of ribbon for the name tags. The two that had the same color would be prayer partners. I made all of the names and poked the holes for the ribbon to be attached. I said a quick prayer over all of them, asking the Lord to place the prayer partners together as He wanted them. Then, I shuffled the tags and simply picked the name tag off the top of the pile, grabbing the ribbon that I had already cut. I didn't look at the names to see who was paired up with whom. I simply placed them all in the bag to be called out at the retreat.

When we all arrived at the retreat house, the first

thing I did was get all of the name tags and call all of the women into the main room. I then called out their names as I pulled the name tags out of the bag. After everyone came forward, I told them to find their prayer partners. Those who had the same color of ribbon would be their prayer partners over the next two and half days of the retreat. I asked them to all spend one hour together immediately and come back together into the main room and share something about their prayer partners that they discovered during the time they spent together. As I stood there watching all of the ladies find their prayer partners, I was thrilled with seeing all of the happy expressions on their faces as they discovered who they were paired up with. Just about the time I was looking at my name tag to see what color I was, Paula walked up to me and said, "Hey Kathryn! It looks like you and I are prayer partners!!" *Can you believe that she ended up being my prayer partner?!* I tried to look excited as I shot up a quick prayer. Ha! God is SO funny to me!

So there we went to spend an hour together. As we walked out to try to find our spot to visit, I began thinking; I should have noticed who I was pairing myself up with! God has a great sense of humor, *doesn't He?*

Over the next hour I began to see Paula in a completely different light. I began to see the beauty that God had knit together in her. She opened up to me in ways I had never expected. She shared with me deeply. I began to see Christ radiating out through her over the next two and half days. God knew what He was doing when I got paired up with Paula. She shared deeply with me, and I was able to share deeply with her as well. I came to know what a beautiful person she was. I came away with a new friend that weekend. I came away learning so much from her; I came away with a sister in Christ. I came away loving this person that I had dreaded in the past.

Over the next year, Bruce and I began the preparation of going into seminary. The day came when Bruce was going to quit his secure position with the Civil Service and go to seminary full time. This was a huge risk financially for us. It was a leap of faith for us! The Sunday after Bruce quit, we were in church and we didn't let on that we had some worries about getting by to anyone. Our two little girls had no idea how tight things were about to get. Paula came up to me and was congratulatory about our getting started with seminary. I never expressed any worry of any kind to her.

---

*"I recognized the look in your eyes today because I live it so much of the time!"*

---

That afternoon the phone rang, and it was Paula. She asked if she could come over in the next thirty minutes or so. I said, "Sure, we'll be here; is everything okay?"

She said, "Yes, I just need to come over." After hanging up, I told Bruce that Paula needed to come over and would be there soon. I said that she would probably need prayer or something. He said, "Alright; is everything okay with her?" I explained that she didn't state the reason for her visit.

Thirty minutes later the door bell rang, and it was

Paula and her son. They were standing at our door with sacks of groceries. They continued to bring in one sack after the other. I couldn't believe how many groceries she was bringing in! Everything from flour, peanut butter, toilet paper, napkins, steak, hamburger meat, soups, and so much more! I couldn't believe it!

When my faith was faltering, wondering how we were going to make it financially through the next several seminary years, God used Paula to strengthen my faith! I wept. She touched my heart in such a way that I don't know if I will ever be able to express it! I remember asking her why she was doing this. She began to explain something to me I shall never ever forget. She said, "Kathryn, I saw a look in your eyes at church today that no one else recognized. I know how it is to live from paycheck to paycheck, and sometimes not make it to the next one!" She went on to say, "I recognized the look in your eyes today because I live it so much of the time!"

> Think how you have instructed many, how you have strengthened feeble hands. Your words have supported those who stumbled; you have strengthened faltering knees.
>
> Job 4:3–4 NIV

As she went to the grocery store after church to do her own personal shopping, the Lord spoke into her. She heard Him speaking to her in such a way that she was unable to ignore. He laid me and my family upon her heart. She felt that He was asking her to trust Him and be a servant. She felt compelled, driven, to buy us groceries. She even said to us that she didn't know how she was going to get by herself, but she wanted to be obedient to the call. It was amazing the joy that the Lord gave her in doing this! I began to cry as she and her son continued to bring all of the groceries into our house. It spoke volumes to me! God spoke to me that day in such a powerful way! *"He speaks... can you hear Him?"*

> So do not fear, for I am with you; do not be dismayed, for I am your God. I will strengthen you and help you; I will uphold you with my righteous right hand.
>
> Isaiah 41:10 NIV

It was God's way of saying to me, "Fear not, I will always provide for all of your needs." It was affirming Bruce's call once again. It deepened our love for Paula. She said that God impressed it upon her heart to buy the groceries for us. She also said, "I have no idea how I am going to make it through to the next paycheck!" This was a leap of faith for her as she was completely obedient to what God was asking of her. He was asking her to put her faith in Him and to trust Him.

---

*She heard Him speaking to her in such a way that she was unable to ignore.*

---

> For I am the LORD, your God, who takes hold of your right hand and says to you, Do not fear; I will help you.
>
> Isaiah 41:13 NIV

She loved giving to us! She got so much out of it, just as we did. God was doing a work in both of us as only He can do! He was speaking to each of us in this moment. Oh, adored one, He is speaking to you now; *can you hear Him?* He wants you to trust Him, love Him, obey Him, and listen to Him! He wants each of us to live passionately! He wants us to know the joy of giving as well as receiving!

God could have used someone in the church who had wealth, but it would not have spoken as loudly to Bruce and me. God used Paula to speak to us, to prove to us His way of letting us know that He knows our needs and to put our trust in Him. He was doing the very same thing with Paula that day. She made it through the month without ever even missing the money! She was blessed.

God places people in our lives who can minister to us in extremely profound and powerful ways. He knows exactly what it takes to make Himself known to us time and time again. He speaks to us in many, various ways. Who has He used in your life when you least expected Him to? Who might you be blocking out, when you should begin dropping the barrier? God is always at work, always for our betterment, and to bring us into fuller relationship to Him. He uses others to bring us to a deeper faith in Him. His timing is always perfect and resonates profoundly! I would surmise that you have had an experience with someone who rubbed you the wrong way. Don't miss out on the opportunity to experience something beyond yourself. These kinds of encounters are orchestrated by God. God also uses your life and experiences and struggles to help another.

# Tuesday night feedings

*In that moment of awkwardness, I was so consumed with myself, and the pride and other thoughts that I was totally missing the love!*

## The God of All Comfort

Praise be to the God and Father of our Lord Jesus Christ, the Father of compassion and the God of all comfort, who comforts us in all our troubles, so that we can comfort those in any trouble with the comfort we ourselves have received from God. For just as the sufferings of Christ flow over into our lives, so also through Christ our comfort overflows.

2 Corinthians 1:3–5 NIV

It was early evening on Tuesday; I happened to be home early from work, and the house was empty. Interestingly, no one had arrived home from school yet. It was peaceful and quiet. I was thinking about when everyone would be coming home and all of the evening events ahead. The doorbell rang, and there stood dear friends from church with a meal for us.

Was this a test? Did I need a lesson in humbleness that I was unaware of? How was I supposed to accept this meal? I so desperately wanted to pay them for it, for all of their trouble, knowing they were busy and honestly didn't have the time to do this. Awkwardness fell upon me, and I clearly heard in my heart, "It's easier to give than to receive." This statement became very real to me. We love to give away the love of our Lord, but when it comes to accepting the love of our Lord, feelings of undeservedness come up. Unworthiness seems to fill our minds and hearts. I want to be a giver not a taker.

If I'm not able to be one who accepts the gift of love, how then can I know that love? How can I truly give that kind of love away if I don't honestly know it fully, if I haven't accepted it fully? I have to accept His love in the various ways that it shows up so that I fully experience His grace, mercy, and love fully! I don't want to miss a bit of His love!

However, in that moment of awkwardness, I was so consumed with myself, pride, and other thoughts that I was totally missing the love! Oh Lord, I pray that we never miss out on the opportunity to experience and express your love fully! Help us to wrap our arms around the gift and the giver of the gift knowing that You are the One giving to us in all of these moments. Help us to see You in others. The next time the doorbell rings and there stands a person, may we see *You* in them. Fill us with awe and thankfulness so that we may be ready to express that rather than embarrassment! Help us, Lord, to know that You are the Great Giver of Life, that You Lord are the Great Nourisher, the Great I Am, who lives to give to us, who lives to love us, who lives so that we might live more fully!

From the fullness of His grace we have all received one blessing after another.

John 1:16 NIV

> *This family of Christ stretches far beyond the walls of your own family.*

God's people are so amazing! I am moved to tears as I recall the love that was poured out upon me and my family during our financially strapped times through those seminary years.

When I think about nourishment, being fed, and all that comes to us when we are cared for, I become awed. If you are reading this and have folks that give to you in unique ways, ways that you may not have thought of as the Lord caring for you, think again. Our God longs to feed us not only physically, but emotionally and spiritually. He uses those folks in our lives to be that for Him.

I was so impressed by the way all of the people in the church became our extended family, full of compassion and care as they recognized our financial struggle during those seminary years. They were family, extending love and support. It is a place where we feel safe in our vulnerability. In most cases we don't ever want people to know of our vulnerabilities. How priceless for us to have this place of refuge and safety in which we are able to share with them. This family of Christ stretches far beyond the walls of your own family. Neither Bruce nor I had family living in the same city. We had all of our families in other cities and states. In today's society, families seem to be spread out across the country. The church has always become our family. We are here for them, and they are here for us.

I'm not sure how the word was spread; it's one of those wonderful holy mysteries that I will always cherish, but somebody planned for a supply of meals to be delivered to us every Tuesday night in order to help us out. From what I have heard, it was to be for an entire year! What happened for us was a two year delivery, 104 weeks of Tuesday night feedings! We would receive meals from some folks we had never met. We would come home from work, and there on our doorstep would be a gift certificate for pizza or some other restaurant. Many times a pizza delivery person would show up at our door. Other times people would come with food in hand and join us for dinner; others wouldn't have time to stay.

> But he said to his disciples, "Have them sit down in groups of about fifty each." The disciples did so, and everybody sat down. Taking the five loaves and the two fish and looking up to heaven, he gave thanks and broke them. Then he gave them to the disciples to set before the people. They all ate and were satisfied, and the disciples picked up twelve basketfuls of broken pieces that were left over.
>
> Luke 9:14–17 NIV

> *Givers are in a position to be able to aid the Father! They are in ministry with the Father, side by side, allowing the Father to meet all the needs of another for His glory! This is such an amazing honor and privilege for givers! They experience the holiness of their endeavor with Him!*

It was such a blessing! We know how busy life is, and to have the added responsibility of bringing or providing us with a meal on Tuesday nights was above and beyond. Some people really went all out and provided five and six course meals! They would provide soups, and salads, and the entrée, and veggies, bread and dessert, all of which they actually baked! We couldn't get over this kind of love and care that was bestowed upon us!

The other blessing was the way that every single time, after every meal we always had enough for leftovers! We were full, and our tummies were satisfied beyond measure! Our hearts were also full from the love that was poured out upon us. We were so thankful! This aided us financially, not only in the one meal but in the way we always had more for other meals! We were thankful and remain so today. This is the kind of gift that remains, because love never leaves; it stays in the heart. Another one of the many ways the Lord speaks His love into us.

The girls were young and always looked forward to those Tuesday nights! They always asked, "Is today Tuesday?" We would answer, "Yes, it sure is," and they would exclaim, "Yeah! We get surprises!" They would look at each other and begin to try to guess what treats would arrive. They loved it! They would even try to guess who would provide the meal. Bruce and I would even get in on the game. It was fun to try to guess, and then upon the arrival of the treasured meal, we would try to see who'd come closest to the correct answer.

This is the way the Lord made His love so real and tangible to us. This caused our girls to have understanding about the way of giving with a pure heart, giving with no strings attached. This also taught them, as well as us, how to receive. This receiving brought about humbleness in us. As I said earlier, we found ourselves needing to be able to get our pride out of the way in order to enable us to walk fully with God in those moments of giving. Giving God's love away is what gives our lives meaning and purpose. When you are to be used for the glory of the Lord, it brings you a new awareness of the way that we are to function as the body.

Givers are in a position to be able to aid the Father! They are in ministry with the Father, side by side, allowing the Father to meet all the needs of another for His glory! This is such an amazing honor and privilege for givers! They experience the holiness of their endeavor with Him!

And my God will meet all your needs according to his glorious riches in Christ Jesus. To our God and Father be glory for ever and ever. Amen.

Phil. 4:19–20 NIV

> *Just because we can be limited in our abilities,*
> *know that He is unlimited in His!*

This provision was a direct answer to our prayers. We prayed that all of our needs would be met as we took our leap of faith upon entering seminary. We prayed that our Lord would give provision to us and that we would recognize it as His provision. God answered those prayers in such a beautiful way.

In talking with many people about prayer, I have heard them say that they felt uncomfortable praying to God for the "little things," as if they were not significant enough to bring before Him. They justified their thinking by saying that they would not want to bother God with the matters of their lives that could keep Him from focusing on the bigger, more important things in the lives of other folks who had more desperate needs. They felt like God was too busy to mess around with these kinds of details of their lives, and they would therefore be troubling Him. This is plainly not true. If God were to answer all of your prayers, it does not mean that He is anything like us, unable to focus on a whole host of things all at once. He is so far beyond what each of us are capable. Just because we can be limited in our abilities, know that He is unlimited in His. We can never drain the resources of His majesty! There is always more where that came from! It is an unending supply of His love and provision! Ask Him for your needs! Get into the relationship with Him that He longs to be in with you! This is precisely why He died for you, because of His extreme love for you! He is a big God and capable of being with each of us all at once. This passage tells us to do so:

> Be anxious for nothing, but in everything by prayer and supplication with thanksgiving let your requests be made known to God.
>
> Philippians 4:6 NASB

Trust this, and live this fully; don't hesitate to *"let your requests be made known to God."* And trust God to meet your need in *His* way, no matter how He chooses to meet your need, and no matter how great or small you think it is. Accept His provision knowing it has come straight from Him!

# STRUGGLE... TAKE IT OR LEAVE IT?

*We honestly felt like we were living (or fighting) in the boxing ring of faith, often feeling beaten, bruised, and battered, just waiting for the bell to ring so that we could finally sit on the corner stool, take a quick breather and get back out there to continue the faith fight.*

(This chapter is dedicated in loving memory to Bishop Leo Alard and to his "extraordinarily real" wife, Aida, and their precious daughter, Rebecca)

Not only so, but we also rejoice in our sufferings, because we know that suffering produces perseverance; perseverance, character; and character, hope. And hope does not disappoint us, because God has poured out his love into our hearts by the Holy Spirit, whom he has given us.

Romans 5:3–5 NIV

We pulled into the parking lot of the Diocesan office to let Bishop Alard know we could take no more. Bruce found a parking space, pulled in and put the car in park, turned the key and pulled it out of the ignition. He looked at me, grabbed my hand, and released a mournful sigh, and he said with the distinct sound of sorrow, and yet his question rang with determination, "Are you ready?"

I looked wearily up at him, and put my free hand over his and said, "I support you all the way. Yep, I'm ready." We took deep breaths, unbuckled our seatbelts, and headed in. Bruce opened the door for me; we walked in gripping each others hands, united in our decision to leave the struggle behind, to quit no matter what.

We began walking up the stairs, heads held high in one moment, and hanging down with extreme sadness in the next. We approached the receptionist and announced that we were there to see Bishop Alard.

The loaded question... Struggle, take it or leave it? What would you do? I am willing to bet that if you are in the midst of the pressure of struggle right now, you want to throw your hands up and say, "Leave it!" In fact, I would also imagine that you've asked God "What in the world are you up to, God?!" We all know it's certainly not much fun going through the tough things; in fact, it can actually cause you to question if God loves you, if He cares, if He even knows you are alive and in such great need. Believe me, I know! There have been many times in the midst of great challenges I have screamed out to God, and questioned His judgment, His methodology, His way of showing love for me muttering sarcastically under my breath to Him that He sure does have a funny way of showing love. At some point along the way we all experience this.

In our life journey thus far one of our many struggles was during seminary.

> *The moment that I step away from Him is when everything becomes impossible in my storm.*

In our weakness and exhaustion we made the decision to give up on seminary. Bruce and I didn't feel like we could continue. For so long we were such great tag team partners in the boxing ring of faith. When I was tired, he would be the one to cheer me on, pick me back up, and when he was the one tired, I'd do the same for him. There came a time when both of us felt as though we'd been beaten, bruised, and were bleeding. We were exhausted, so tired we didn't think we could continue on.

In our weakness we'd made the decision to quit seminary. We rationalized that we could continue to serve the Lord in many other ways. Bruce has dyslexia and keeping up the pace was beyond difficult for him. The reading was never done, with two hundred or more pages to read nightly, twenty-page papers to write, be a devoted husband and dad, and experiencing the emotional drain with the pressures of not providing financially for the family. These are just a few of the struggles during that time.

Both of us completely drained spiritually, financially, and emotionally, we made the decision to quit, give up. We called the office of Bishop Leo Alard to make an appointment with him to let him know we could go no further. We were living in Austin, and the appointment was made for us to meet him in his Houston office. Leo had no idea that we were coming to tell him of our exhaustion, and to leave the struggle behind. He thought our visit was going to be one of the regular visits that Bruce as a seminarian had to make.

After making our drive from Austin to Houston and letting the receptionist know we were there to see Leo, we sat and waited for a few minutes. We whispered to each other as we waited, both of us making sure this was it; that we both were in agreement about giving up. I remember Bruce saying to me, "No matter what he says, we are quitting. Nothing can change our minds, right?"

"Right! We are done," I said.

We reminded each other of our exhaustion and reassured each other that we were making the right decision to quit. We both thanked each other for all we'd been through together in this process.

Our attention was immediately shifted to the glorious smile and enthusiastic greetings of love and welcome from our dear, dear friend, Leo! His arms outstretched as big as he could stretch ready to embrace us with his huge hug! No one could hug quite like Leo! He was Cuban and had the voice of the Godfather! His voice was unmistakable and so full of love and joy! He hugged us both and told us how happy he was to see us! Walking back to his office, we shared in idle chit chat about his wonderful wife, Aida, and precious daughter, Rebecca, and about our daughters, Tabitha and Kellie Ann. We were catching up on each others lives, and on his travels.

Dyslexia was the main culprit in our decision-making process regarding seminary. Bruce has struggled with this his entire life. It made keeping up with the reading and the writing impossible. It caused him to feel incompetent and inept, which was taking a toll on him in more ways than we felt we could continue to bear.

> *Ready to get back out there in our boxing ring of faith, we felt like champions!*

As we sat down in Leo's office, he began to apologize for the difficult time that he knew Bruce was having. He said that he kept Bruce in his daily prayers, and saw Bruce as one of his heroes. He proceeded to tell us why. He told us of his daughter, Rebecca, who had been diagnosed with dyslexia, and that for her to get through high school would be an amazing feat, and that those in "expert positions" said she would never get into college, and here Bruce was pursuing his Masters in Divinity and ordination! He continued to apologize that the seminary didn't allow for any kind of aid or any kind of relaxation in regard to his learning disability. He said in his passionate Godfather voice, "Bruce, You, you my brave, courageous man, you are the plow, you are the one to go before all the others that have learning disabilities, and you prepare the way for those like my daughter, Rebecca! I trust and know that she will go to college! You, Bruce, are one who is shedding the blood, sweat and tears in order to make it possible for others to make it through seminary! You make me so proud! I see you as a man of strength, and honor sitting here before me, and you make me a better man for knowing you! I admire your strength, and your desire to press on no matter what it takes! You are no quitter! I stand in awe and have such respect for you, Bruce!" His arms spoke fully with passion as he lifted Bruce (and me) up!

Then Leo turned to me and said, "Kathryn, I see a woman who loves her husband, who is so proud of her husband! I see a woman who loves the Lord, and a woman who is faithful in the ways you support him! You two will make a wonderful couple in ministry just as my wife and I have!" He told us of his struggles and how he has had to overcome them, and how they caused him to be a better priest, and caused him to never take his calling for granted!

There we sat, obviously feeling more called to stay than to quit! Neither of us dared to tell him why we came. We walked out of that office with a new perspective, a new way of thinking about our struggle, with a renewed passion for the calling. We had a new passion in the way that our calling was reaffirmed that day. Walking out of the office, we felt as though we were walking on clouds! So high and lifted up! *He speaks... can you hear Him?"*

Back in the car, sitting in the parking lot, Bruce

looked at me and said, "What happened to *no matter what?*"

I said, "I couldn't say anything after that! Why didn't you say anything?" We laughed and we laughed and we laughed! Then we cried with such reverence and gratefulness unto our Lord, God.

This is the evidence of the verse above that proves *God has poured out his love into our hearts by the Holy Spirit, whom He has given us!* The is one of the ways He reaches down into our lives and pours out his love upon us, like grace raining on us, washing us, reviving us!

> *God spoke to us that day through Leo. He Speaks...*
> *Can You Hear Him?*

Sometimes in the whisper of the wind, or the cries of a baby, through a wise one He has placed in your life... listen, always listen, He speaks personally to you each and every day. Are you listening? I promise you He is speaking!

You never know how one person's struggle can minister to you, or how your struggle can minister to another and bring comfort and peace along the way!

During the seminary years we experienced financial stress, the pressure of my being the main bread winner, raising the girls, the academic struggle of the seminary trials that were almost more than what we could endure.

I have learned the above Scripture to be true, completely true. I know that when it says to "rejoice" in our sufferings, it sounds absolutely absurd! I will be the first one to admit that in this present day I am not fully capable of doing that all of the time. I am capable of it more today than years past, through Christ. Each of us is going to have at least one kind of stormy struggle come into our lives. It is what it is. It is for a reason, and a good reason. The moment that I step away from Him is when everything becomes impossible in my storm. Stay close to Him even in the storm, *especially* in the storms, cling to Him, and never, ever forget this! This is the most important thing for you to remember. Even in your fear, your anger, your pain, cling to Him! As you cling to Him during the storm, you draw nearer to Him in ways that you wouldn't otherwise. You will begin to hear His voice; you will begin to experience His love as He grows your faith and your perseverance, your character, and last but not least, your hope in those things to come!

Our hope, our calling was to come, and has come! Bruce doesn't take this position lightly. He honors it, he cherishes the church, he loves the church even when it can drive him crazy! Ha!! Even if you are called to something, it doesn't mean it will be easy, but you will learn perseverance, your character will be built and you will truly know about the hope of things to come!

Let's take a look at Joseph and some of his struggles. Those of you that know me have heard me say that Joseph is my most favorite person in the Bible! In fact I love both Josephs! The Joseph I am referring to here is the son of Jacob. You talk about a man of honor, character, and perseverance, and one of hope of things to come!

You talk about struggle, boy, did he experience struggle! He was disowned by his very own brothers because of their jealousy toward him, and sold into slavery. He was accused of something he did not do, and because of that, imprisoned wrongly for years! All the while, continuing to trust and honor the Lord God. What I love about Joseph is that he is a regular guy just like you and me. You may think, yeah, but God's hand was upon Joseph. And you would be absolutely right; God's hand was upon Joseph.

> *The only huge part you are missing is that God's hand is also upon you!*

We all have been placed in some sort of leadership role, whether we are a witness in our behavior, in an executive level position, as a facilitator of a Sunday school class, as a parent, as a co-worker, it matters not. What does matter is not only *what* you have been through, but *how* you've been going through it. During these trials do you tend to lean on yourself or to lean on the Lord? Whatever storm you are currently facing, allow it to produce the character of God in you.

So many times when we look at the characters in the Bible or those folks around us, we can seem to have this preconceived notion that God's hand is upon everyone else, and not ourselves! It's simply not true. God is in love with each of us, and that includes *you!* The question is... Are you in love with Him? I want you to realize that the Bible is to bring us hope, is to help us to know that our lives, our hurts, our pain, our hopes and dreams are not unlike theirs in the Bible. The more we get in touch with the Word, the more we get in touch with God. As John 1:1 says, *In the beginning was the Word, and the Word was with God, and the Word was God.* Do not be afraid to start studying the Bible. Don't view it as too complicated to understand. Instead, open the pages with faith in knowing that the Lord wants you to know Him, and go at it with that kind of knowing. When I first began studying the Word, I wondered if I would ever understand it. You never will if you don't start. The moment you start is the hardest, and it gets easier with each study you progress in. We begin to understand Him through the study of His Word, and we are able to mature in our faith walk, in our journey with Him.

Getting back to Joseph, he could have easily been one that ended up bitter, but that was not his way. He chose not to be bitter. He chose to love, to be a man of honor and grace. His story is one of the most beautiful demonstrations of true forgiveness. When he was reunited with his brothers, who staged his death to look as though he'd been killed by wild animals, when they had actually sold him into slavery, he had complete love and forgiveness toward them. He could have chosen not to forgive. He could have chosen to be hardhearted, and a very angry bitter man. He would have been justified to be full of hate and anger. How do you think the story would have been different if Joseph had not been a man of honor, and integrity, and trusting God? Think about that. Are you currently allowing your circumstances to cause you to be bitter? You do realize that you have the ability to choose here, don't you? You absolutely do! God has given you that kind of powerful freedom! Each choice you make creates an outcome. Pray about this, meditate on it, and allow Him in; allow the trials to be viewed in a new way, inviting God in to calm the seas, to build your character.

Keep coming back to Joseph when you think about your tribulation. Joseph's struggle went on for *thirteen* excruciating years! But what I love so much about Joseph (can you tell he is one of my most favorite characters in the Bible?) is that he didn't seem to be focused on the bad hand he was dealt. He found his joy in helping others around him while imprisoned, which I believe is one of the things that gave him reason to continue on, and this provided him with joy. As you read through his life while in prison, you read about how he continued to keep his trust in the Lord. God honored this and caused him to step into leadership positions when he was a slave, when he was a prisoner, and amazingly through all that, he became the ruler of all Egypt! All of what he'd been through prepared him to be in such a position.

*God is in love with each of us, and that includes you! The question is... Are you in love with Him?*

I'm sure that being imprisoned for so many years, he from time to time would lose hope. You can just imagine the thoughts he could have had about how his brothers had ruined his life, the thoughts of Potiphar's wife telling the most horrible lies about him, ruining his reputation and having him placed in prison for so long. Thoughts of never getting out, thoughts that no one cared, thoughts that he didn't even matter, that he'd been completely forgotten. As he served others in spite of his circumstances, this was when he'd hear the voice of the Lord, reminding him that he did matter, and was loved. The same is for you in your struggle; you begin to hear our Lord's voice telling you that you do matter, that you are loved by the Most High God! None of these people stopped God from bringing Joseph into his destiny! Remember that when you think someone has completely ruined something for you; trust that if this is Gods will for you, if it's your destiny, the Lord will bring it to pass. Remember that. Persevere, trust, pray, and hope. Keep doing life the righteous way; keep honoring God through it all; your reward is sure.

I know a woman who has the most beautiful, tender heart, whose name is Shirley. Shirley grew up with polio and had eighteen surgeries. She was in a brace or a cast all the way up to her hips; she had limited movement for much of her life. Shirley could not do the things other children and young adults could do! I never knew her as a child with this disease. I've only known her as an adult and knowing her now, I know of her magnificence! She says and believes that her polio was a gift! There are many who could have taken these very circumstances and taken an opposite view. She could have ended up a very bitter woman, and we as a society would have thought she had the right to be because of her polio.

Today she is a massage therapist, bringing her healing touch to those in pain. She believes that she has been given compassion to impart upon those in her care. She knows that God has created her to be a beautiful, therapeutic healer.

Shirley tells me that she would never want to be rid of her struggle. She says that during the times while in a cast and not able to go and play with the other kids, it was a time for her to dream, a time of hope for her. How wonderful this is! Had she not been through this, she would not have this or know this. She knew that she had angels all around her in the many surgeries, and says that she had them with her and knew Jesus was always there holding her hand. She was given dreams (as was Joseph), dreams with Jesus walking with her, with braces on her legs, telling her that she was going to be okay. Our Lord was making Himself known to her, and she was very aware of that. *"He Speaks... Can You Hear Him?"*

*Allow the voice of the Lord to speak into your heart if you have been keeping Him at bay.*

Even though she has one leg smaller with many scars, she knows of the gift of life. She knows she was able to hear Him, and He reassured her that she was going to be a beautiful person, even though in her growing up she wanted to hide her scars, she heard Him say she was beautiful. And I know her; she is beautiful!

*He speaks... Can you hear Him?* Are you listening?

The Lord has created us to live into freedom. He has given us freedom of thought, the freedom of choice, the freedom to believe, the capacity to be thinking, feeling human beings! What freedoms we have! What a beautiful thing this freedom of thought is and how powerful it is! The place where we find true freedom is when we are in His will. His will for us is perfect. His will for us is *always* with our very best interest in mind. When we are choosing this for our lives, we experience full freedom, full joy!

What are you doing with your mind? Do you fill it with the holy things of the Lord; especially in the trying times of the storm? Your mind and your body are the temple of the Lord. What ways are you choosing to live your life? What thoughts, what disposition do you want or do you long for? Think about the way you are in the times of struggle. Think about what the Lord has taught you, how He's grown you, drawn you closer to Him, matured your Christian walk. This journey of life is exactly that, a journey. We were created to walk in relationship with Christ with every step. When we veer off into another direction, it is our choice. Much of this journey is made up of our thoughts.

In my journey I have always tried to see everyone in a positive light, and be a positive light to those I encounter. It's my choice to see and experience beauty fully. It is my choice to enjoy each and every human being I encounter, no matter how different they might be. The

Lord has taught me to do this without naivety. I am able to discover and uncover the beauty within them that the Lord has created. This is my choice to do so, and I find it to serve me well. I find it to bring much beauty and joy to my life. Choices are amazing. We make so many every day! With every choice there is a consequence. With good choices we experience good or great consequences. With bad choices we experience bad or horrible consequences. We become attuned to these outcomes *or we don't*. I would encourage you to begin really thinking, examining the choices you make and why you make them. They form patterns in your life. What patterns are you forming through your choices? Begin to pray about this in your life, and become more aware of the way you are allowing the Lord to mold and shape you, choosing to be in alignment with the way the Lord wants to shape your life. Are you walking with Him or against Him? We have been given complete free will to choose not to do the will of God, but the one certain thing we can never ever get away from are the consequences of our choices.

Struggles, hmmm, yes, I'm honestly grateful for them. Not that I have enjoyed the struggle itself... but do enjoy the fruit from it. The passage at the beginning of this chapter from Romans 5 is true; the struggle really does produce perseverance, and causes me to think about my choices and the outcomes of them. It causes me to know that the Lord has created me to be faithful and to press on toward the goal. The perseverance in and of itself is character building.

Perhaps you have felt imprisoned in one way or another much like Joseph did, or in a physical way like Shirley, or in ways similar to Bruce and me. Trust the

trial; trust that you are in the process of character building, being shaped by the Potter. Be aware of how you
choose to view it; be aware that you stand in choice here.
Even if it seems there is one storm after the other, choose
your faith, knowing that the Lord is doing a work in you.
Don't allow anything, anyone, or any thoughts to keep
you from completing the work the Lord has called you
to. This is where your hope comes, knowing that a good
thing is imminent. Allow the Lord to show you His perspective, as you keep yourself in His Word, keeping your
trust in Him and your heart with His. All the while you
continue building character and a love relationship with
the Lord.

Struggle, take it or leave it? What have you been
shown through yours? What would you change? What
wisdom have you gained? Where have you been able to
look back and see exactly what the Lord was showing
you?

> I thank my God every time I remember you. In all
> my prayers for all of you, I always pray with joy be-
> cause of your partnership in the gospel from the first
> day until now, being confident of this, that he who
> began a good work in you will carry it on to comple-
> tion until the day of Christ Jesus.
>
> Philippians 1:3–6 NIV

I have learned and am thankful for the other gifts
that come along with our struggles; the way the Lord has
presented folks along the way to speak into my life, my
heart and soul. He has a way of caring for us and sending
us the faith we need when ours is lacking.

# So this is what walking by faith is!

Fear knocked at the door, Faith answered. No one was there.

—Ancient Inscription

> *When we allow our fears to keep us from stepping out in faith to what the Lord has called us to, that is where our life-long disappointments live.*

I read this somewhere years ago and scribbled it down because it resonated with me; it speaks about the power of fear and how fear pursues after us. Subsequently, it speaks to the greater power of faith which makes the fear dissipate.

> _We all have entered this life with a
> God-given purpose!_

Learning to replace fear with faith is the key to having our fears dissipate by means of walking by faith. Failure is never striving to do what we recognize in our heart of hearts God is calling us to! When we allow our fears to keep us from stepping out in faith to what the Lord has called us to, that is where our life-long disappointments live. If God is calling you to something, He obviously knows without a shadow of a doubt that you are capable or He never would have called you to it. When we live into what God has called us to, that is when and where we find our great joy! That is when we are fully in step with Him, living out our purpose! Go for the gold. Here is where your boxing ring of faith comes in again; your fears are something within that need to be fought with faith in order to live fully into your dreams, hopes, passions, and God given destiny!

Too many of us cut the meaning and purpose of our lives short because we fear failure. It's like sleep-walking through life, and needing to be re-awakened to the phenomenal possibilities that God has for us so that we step into the living color. God-given dreams were planted in each of our souls before we were born!

Meditate on the passage below:

Oh yes, You shaped me first inside, then out; You

formed me in my mother's womb. I thank You, High God-You're breathtaking! Body and soul, I am marvelously made! I worship in adoration- what a creation! You know me inside and out, you know every bone in my body; You know exactly how I was made, bit by bit, how I was sculpted from nothing into something. Like an open book, you watched me grow from conception to birth; all the stages of my life were spread out before you, The days of my life all prepared before I'd even lived one day. Your thoughts- how rare, how beautiful! God, I'll never comprehend them! I couldn't even begin to count them- any more than I could count the sand of the sea. Oh, let me rise in the morning and live always with you!

Psalm 139:13–17 MSG

We all have entered this life with a God-given purpose! Take the journey of faith to discover what awaits you just over the horizon! Be *alive,* be *fulfilled,* be *awakened* to the possibilities of God!

When we are afraid of failure, we are totally focused on ourselves and cannot be focused on the Lord. The reason I can speak so candidly about this is because I know it too well. I hate to admit it, but boy, do I know it. The idea of writing this book was so very scary. It is through the encouragement of family and friends and my Life Coach whom God has placed in my life that He began to speak to me. These people held me accountable to what God had given me to do. It is through His strength that I am able, not my own strength, AND it has brought me such joy. If we are relying on the Most High

God, the King of Kings, and the Lord of Lords, we have nothing to fear. The moment that I begin doing things in my own strength (which, by the way, is far more often than I care to admit) is when it falls apart.

---

*Be a faith-walker rather than a fear-walker!*

---

Hebrews Chapter 11 speaks of faith and actually gives us a definition of what faith is:

> Now faith is being sure of what we hope for and certain of what we do not see. This is what the ancients were commended for. By faith we understand that the universe was formed at God's command, so that what is seen was not made out of what was visible.
>
> Hebrews 11:1–3 NIV

> And without faith it is impossible to please God, because anyone who comes to Him must believe that He exists and that He rewards those who earnestly seek him.
>
> Hebrews 11:6 NIV

Okay, let's get our egos out of the way here; let's be sure to make our faith about Him, not about ourselves! When we make it about ourselves, that's the very moment when we mess it all up! Take Peter: when he was walking on water and focused on Christ, he was doing it!

The moment he took his eyes off of Christ, he was going down! Thank God the Lord is there for us to look back to! Thank God He time after time draws us back to Himself! This happens when we take our eyes off of the Lord, and we will time and time again! I know because I have, and I sadly still do; this is when we are going down! There is a reason for this, and it is because the Lord wants us to look at Him, rely upon Him not ourselves. He wants us to bring glory to Him, not to ourselves. He wants us to glorify Him.

According to verse one, we must begin our faith journey with hope in Him. To me when I try to wrap my brain around this, it tells me that I must have some sort of want, longing, purpose—a want for something more, something to come, and something not yet seen. When you begin to experience the desire for something more, it is because you are innately yearning to please God. He wired us to want to please Him, and when we do, that is when we experience our greatest pleasure. Again, this is how He has made us. When you begin to notice that yearning for more meaning, more purpose, the need for fulfillment, begin looking at where you are lacking in pleasing Him. If you find yourself thinking there has to be more *to* me, there has to be more *for* me, it is the time for you to go to His throne and begin praying about it, to begin talking to the Lord about it. Take this question to the Father who spoke the universe into being. Go deeply into conversation with Him. Go prayerfully with your want. Beth Moore said something in one of her studies that has stayed with me for some time now: in your conversations with God, come right out and tell Him—"God, I WANT this thing you've given me!" He knows you do, and He wants you to want to tell Him, He wants to give you those things that are in His will for you! He also wants to protect you from those things that you may *think* you want, but that are not His will for you.

> *Our Lord God spoke all of this creation into being! This is only a tiny part of His creativity.*

When the Lord first gave me this book to write, I was so afraid of it that I ignored it for quite some time. I knew that He'd called me to it, and many times wish I hadn't heard Him speak it into me. God has a way of continuing to remind you of what He wants you to do. He'll have others bring it up and ask you things like, "So, how's that book coming along?" *"He speaks... can you hear Him?"* When you read this, the Lord is probably reminding you of something he has been nudging you to do for Him right this very second! Sometimes we feel so incapable, so scared that we are not going to perform as well as so-and-so, allowing that to keep us from our calling! Oh, how you just want it to go away, and in the same breath you want it so badly you hate to admit to yourself! It's crazy the way we have it roll around in our heads and allow the fear to keep us from going for it. Be a faith-walker rather than a fear- walker!

During the process of writing this book, I lost it twice! It completely disappeared; it wasn't on the hard drive, either! Gone! I was beside myself, full of anxiety and frustration. It was 4:44 in the morning the first time it happened. The Lord had awakened me to write in the wee hours of the morning as He so often does, and I was typing away, I was on a roll and experiencing a wonderful flow. I was continuously pushing "save" and enjoying the quiet. I push "save" about every five minutes so as not to lose anything.

Well, I pushed something, and I lost the entire book! All of it! I began trying to find it, doing a search, feeling my heart begin to rush, heat rising into my chest and neck when it was appearing as though it was nowhere to be found.

This is where I found myself speaking out, crying out, truly acknowledging for the first time, *God, I want this!* I know it was You who gave it to me! I know that I have often felt it was a burden! Oh God, Oh God, I'm so sorry I've sometimes felt that way! God, I love it! I love this gift!

Wow! What a realization! By this time I'd gone in and awakened Bruce in a bit of a panic, not a full-fledged panic, but definitely feeling like crying. Mind you, it's very early, and he doesn't have a clue as to what my upset is. Bruce is the kind of guy when he wakes up in the morning, who heads straight to the kitchen for his cup of hot tea. He needs caffeine before he gets real revved up! But he is hearing panic in my voice, and he's definitely hearing the tears behind my vocal cords. I can imagine that all he's thinking is, *"Must fix, not a good sound, must fix, must make this noise stop..."* I giggle now as I write this because I love Bruce so much. I love the way he wants everything to always be okay for me. He truly does. I always wake up each morning with cheer; he's used to that. It's comfortable for him; he calls me "Morning Star" because of the way I awaken each morning. We both wake up so completely different from each other!

So, Bruce stumbles into our office and begins trying to figure out what my problem is and how he can fix it, and fix it fast! I explain, and pace the floor in tears. Bruce sits down at my computer and fumbles around, searching for the lost file. As he does, I am talking with God in a blend of what I'll call a panicky calm. I start saying, "*Lord, You spoke this book into me, You are the One who gave it to me, I never asked for it!*"

It was in this moment that I realized that I loved it! That I loved the gift of it! I began to thank Him for the first time for this gift! It is when I began to realize that it was a gift! I had to tell Him I wanted it, and that I realized it *was* part of my purpose, my calling! I no longer was simply being obedient to it, but now loving it, and embracing it, because of His gloriousness!

*Do you have faith that He is capable of speaking into your life?*

Given to me by Him, and it was now *gone!* I began on this journey knowing of His majesty.

This is where we begin with Him, in obedience. Notice I said, this is where we *begin,* where we get started in our love journey with Him. We go in the beginning because He somehow has revealed a calling upon us. It may be to step out into the area of teaching a Bible study; starting a ministry within your church, starting your own business... we timidly begin to do it mainly out of obedience. Many times this is the way we begin living into our calling, our purpose, our destiny, through simple obedience. There may even be fear, some doubt, and even some irritation toward it in the beginning. As you begin doing the work He's placed before you, getting involved with it, you begin learning it, feeling more and more connected to it. Then there comes a point where you are no longer looking at the surface of it. You begin to go deeper into the heart of it, become truly involved with it, and love it. In this time of almost losing the book, I found my treasure in it; I gained it back a hundred-fold, no longer just obedient to it!

It's comparable to the ocean. The ocean is full of life when we look beneath the surface of it! We can't see the true beauty of it until we submerge ourselves into the depths of it. I can look out across the ocean and can see water for miles and miles. I am awed by the beauty of the surface, and I haven't even begun peering into the depths of it! Let's go deeper here; let's go under. What is down there? There is living, breathing plant life and the most amazing sea creatures living together in community. The beauty of the coral and the home it provides to the sea creatures! The animals of the sea are created with such splendor! There are seahorses, the neon blue starfish, the stingray, the crab, the many rainbow-colored fish, dolphins, whales, seals, the seaweed, the reefs, the sea lilies, and all the different aquatic blooms! Is God an artist or what! Our Lord God *spoke* all of this creation into being! This is only a tiny part of His creativity.

God had given me something beautiful, and I was seeing the surface of it until it was gone! It was in that moment that I saw further into it, I then realized I loved what He'd given me, and saw the beauty in it. I *now wanted* what He'd spoken into me to do! I am no longer doing it out of obedience! I am now doing it for the love He's given me for it!

Do you have faith that He is capable of speaking into your life? Think on these things, believe on these things. Begin your faith by asking Him to speak into your life the gift of hope, the gift of your purpose. As you do, commit to being faithfully and earnestly obedient to it because that is how your passion and love for what He's called you to grows into His beautiful creation. Remember what verse 6 of the Hebrews 11 passage says, *"And without faith it is impossible to please God,"* and listen to the last half of the verse, *"because anyone who comes to Him must believe that He exists and that He rewards those who earnestly seek Him."*

> *The love of the Lord is always enough if you are deeply connected, deeply and faithfully rooted in that love.*

We are shown in the verse above that we must be earnest seekers, to go deeper, just as one who wants to see the beauty below the ocean depth must begin by snorkeling in the ocean. This is where faith lives; begin to go a bit deeper. This is what we must do as well when it comes to getting into the true walk of faith. We must open our Bibles and get into the Word so that it by the Holy Spirit may be revealed into our souls at a level that is deeper than what it has been in the past.

Join a Bible study group so that you can glean insight from others, and so that you will be held accountable to do the reading of Scripture. You will begin to find the deep treasure you have been hunting for! You will begin to know God! Imagine knowing someone of His magnitude! What an honor it is, and what a privilege it is! You are invited to join Him, you know. You don't have to be a member of some elite club His doors are open, wide open!

As you begin the process of knowing God, you will be given the keys to the Kingdom. Your life becomes new each day. You then begin to not only snorkel, but you will become more faithful, and less fearful, as you begin to go deeper in your faith; you'll start scuba diving! In doing so you find the brilliance in the treasures of the deep!

Let's look at Hebrews 11, verse 1: "*Now faith is being sure of what we hope for and certain of what we do not see.*"

Now this is not really so hard, I've heard people say that it's hard to believe in God when you cannot see Him. It's all about the perspective that you take. To me it's the exact opposite, when I take in and survey the surroundings just in my little corner of the world, I see things that cause me to KNOW there is a God, because of the incredible creation all around me. It screams out His presence!

Here the Scripture is calling you to be aware of "what we do not see." This is to become aware of and believe in the "something else", the invisibleness, yet obviously visible Holy Spirit. There are truths that cannot be seen with the naked eye and yet are revealed by creation itself. Some of these things cannot be touched physically, but can be touched and felt inwardly and spiritually.

> *Do you realize the agelessness of the Holy Spirit?*
> *Have you ever really thought about this?*

What are "the things hoped for?" In most of us it is the depth for which we long. The spiritual depth to be living into our purpose, to be the persons that we want to be is truly what we long after. We long to be ones of peace, of joy, of love, of forgiveness, of gentleness, of faithfulness, of kindness, of patience and self-control. God has wired us to desire these things as they are all fruits of the Spirit, and they become a natural part of who we are when we are walking in faith, in connection with our Lord.

Many times if we are not getting the things hoped for in the proper way, we will "act out" in a way that is not healthy. For instance, if a man or a woman is longing for love and not receiving it in a healthy way, he or she will go in search of it in the wrong way and reap the uncomfortable consequences. The love of the Lord is always enough if you are deeply connected, deeply and faithfully rooted in that love.

"You can keep a faith only as you can keep a plant, by rooting it into your life and making it grow there."– Phillips Brooks

Chapter 11 of Hebrews is one faith story after another. Each story is different from the other. Just as you and I have our different faith stories, we all can say that we have our faith in Him to do the many wondrous, miraculous things that He calls us to. What is amazing to me is that our God has faith in us! He calls us to walk into ministry with Him, believing in us to do those things! If the almighty God believes in us, don't you think we'd be wise to also? It would be foolish of us not to. Let's make it a point to begin trusting Him; He obviously trusts you and me to be able to accomplish what He appoints us to. That is such a remarkable thought, a surprising realization!

Take a look through Hebrews Chapter 11; almost every paragraph begins with "By faith..." and it's a story of those stepping fully into faith. Reading these passages you will be shown and taught about faith and the relationship of it to God. In my study Bible the title of Chapter 11 denotes what the chapter is about and reads "By Faith." In verse 4 of chapter 11, it says, "*By faith* Abel offered God a *better* sacrifice than Cain did." To me when I break this out further, this passage is giving us such wonderful direction! It is pointing us to the fact that our living by faith is far better than the opposite. Two verses later in verse 6, we learn of the importance of faith. It tells us, "And without faith it is impossible to please God, because anyone who comes to Him must believe that He exists and that He rewards those who earnestly seek Him."

Walking by faith... step by faithful step. Each step is a step of intention. Faith is where everything happens! Take a look at chapter 11 a bit further, and you will notice the past heroes of the faithful. You will witness how it translates to you today. By faith Abel–by faith Enoch–by faith Noah–by faith Abraham–by faith Isaac–by faith Jacob–by faith Moses–by faith the people–by faith the prostitute, Rahab... the list of imperfect people continues up to now. Place your name here, say it out loud. By faith (your name). Wow! Do you recognize how powerful it is for you to be able to continue in this faithful heritage? It belongs to you and me as well! Faith is the belief in knowing the limitless possibilities with our Great Creator. Faith is where we trust that miracles happen. Faith is holy. Our faith is in Him, not in ourselves. Faith in the Holy One. Faith that He has only your good in mind. Faith with eyes on Him in the storm. Faith in action.

Faith is the knowingness that the Holy Spirit lives in me, takes up residence in me. Trusting the wisdom of the Holy Spirit! The Holy Spirit is truly remarkable and absolutely amazing! Do you realize the *agelessness* of the Holy Spirit? Have you ever really thought about this? This to me is the most amazing thing about walking with Christ, making each step a step of faith. Faith is an amazing thing. It's the risk, and yet it's even riskier *not* to have total trust and faith. It is belief in the unknown, yet somehow known. When you step out into faith, you know that you are headed somewhere grand, yet not fully knowing what it will be. You know that you are headed out with faith held tight, gripping on to it so that you don't let it go. Trusting that once you step out, the winds of the Holy Spirit will propel you along! If you never take the step of faith you can not experience the soaring!

It's a choice to actually step into faith and walk by faith. What will you choose? What will be different if you choose not to? The really wonderful question is what will be different if you choose to?

*Join me in a prayer of thanks...*

*God of faithfulness, Oh how I thank you that you have such belief in me. God, I marvel at Your love for me. Let me begin today, right here, right now to begin my journey of faith with dissipating fear, so that eventually any unhealthy fear no longer has a place in my life. God, I want to be a faith-walker, walking boldly into what You have called me to, giving You all glory, honor and praise! Thank You for giving me the precious gift of faith, and for the ability for this gift of faith to continue to grow bigger and bigger in me as I grow closer and closer to You! Amen*

# WE WANT TO CALL HIM DAD

---
※
---

> *As we age, we gain wisdom and insight from our past foolhardiness.*

O h Dad, you are so funny!" one of the girls would exclaim from time to time, or during special moments, "Dad! Carving pumpkins is so much fun!" Trying it on... seeing how it felt... did it fit? Did it land okay? Was it accepted? Would it be rejected? How do we do this? It was a way for them to step forward in faith, even if it did mean the possibility of rejection.

> *Our failures are a huge part of our learning to be successful.*

During the first four years of our marriage, both girls

would be in the midst of doing something with Bruce. It was in the moments that they would be doing things together such as carving a pumpkin, learning to ride a bike, tossing a baseball, learning to bat, building volcanoes as a science project, asking for money, being rescued from sitting on an ant pile with bites everywhere and desperate cries of pain, being in the hospital with the fright of major surgery looming, riding in an ambulance... oh, the list goes on and on of the things we went through as their parents.

The girls, both of them in many of these various kinds of activities, would say Dad, rather than Bruce. In doing so they were trying to convey the love they had for Bruce, the respect they had for him, the faith they were beginning to have in this fatherly relationship with him. They in their own way were calling him this as a high honor, showing that he'd earned the right in their lives to be their Dad.

Each time they did, Bruce would gently and lovingly reply to them, "You can call me Bruce; I am your parent, and I love you; however, you have a Dad, and I'm not trying to replace him. Your dad and I both love you very much."

Little did we know at the time that they viewed this as a form of rejection. We honestly never thought about it this way. We thought and still do think that he handled that with great care and great love and with respect to their father.

They would continue to do this, and Bruce would continue with the same response over the four years.

Four years into our marriage the girls came to me and told me that they needed to talk to me alone. We sat down, and Tabitha and Kellie Ann began to tell me that they felt like they had two dads and that they wanted to call Bruce Dad.

At this time the girls were approximately eight and eleven years old, with good heads on their shoulders. I questioned them further and said that this was a serious thing, and we had much to consider. I asked them about their real dad and how this might make him feel, and asked how they'd want to let him know. They said that they had already thought about it, and they would just give him a call and tell him. They didn't want to ask him; they wanted to tell him because they had already made the decision.

The next point I brought up was that the tongue was quick to speak in anger, pointing out that when they are angry or frustrated with me, they don't call me Kathryn, and that they continue to call me mom and don't say things in anger like, "You aren't my mom!" further explaining that this could be a very hurtful thing to do to Bruce. Things said in anger can be so damaging, and you can regret those things.

When words are many, sin is not absent, but he who holds his tongue is wise.

Proverbs 10:19 NIV

*Sometimes, years later is when I would actually be able to trace the fingerprints of God, be able to see where the hand of God had been moving all the while.*

They can be forgiven but the pain can still reside. The regret that they could have from doing so could become a heavy burden to them as well. We really talked a lot about the way that we can hurt others with our words. We talked about how the statement of "Sticks and stones may break my bones, but words will never hurt me" is simply not true, explaining what I meant by comparing it to a time when a friend had said something to them that hurt their feelings. They were able to recall the things said by friends readily, proving the lasting effect of the hurt caused. They understood how the person who said those things really wasn't being "good" when they said them. They were so eager to call him Dad that they both made promises that they would try not to do that. This was very important for them. I wasn't aware of how important.

The thing that they said next was what really surprised me and something that I'd never thought about before. They said, "Mom, we want to be there, but we want you to tell him that we want to call him Dad, because every time that we've called him Dad, he always tells us not to call him that, to call him Bruce because we already have a dad. We don't want him to say that to us anymore; we *want* him to *want* us to call him Dad." I asked them how that made them feel when he'd said that to them. They said that it made them feel kind of very bad inside, and made them feel sort of embarrassed that they'd tried to call him that. They said that it also made them feel like maybe he didn't want to be their dad. That's when I realized that they were experiencing the deep pain of rejection, each time he was giving them that gentle reminder of their biological dad, and his rightful place. It was in that moment when I realized they had felt rejected each time he said that to them and that pained me deeply! I felt horrible, knowing how much Bruce loved them. He would have never, ever wanted them to feel anything but full acceptance and love from him.

This was eye-opening for me! I had no idea that they were feeling this way. I reassured them that Bruce did consider them his children and that he saw them as gifts from God, that they were an answer to his prayers, and he did consider himself their dad and their parent.

They said, "Mom, will you be the one to tell him with us?" I said that I would. The three of us went to Bruce and told him that we needed to talk. I explained that the girls had come to me and had something that they wanted to tell him, and that they'd already talked to me, and that the two of them had given this a lot of thought before they had talked to me.

They shared their hearts with him. He listened without saying, "You can call me Bruce..." He heard, he understood completely with his eyes filling with tears as he experienced their love for him in such a beautiful way. In the same moment they experienced the love he had for them in just the same way. God is so good!

---

*This faith doesn't occur overnight, but it does day by day, step by faithful step.*

---

Whoever welcomes one of these little children in my name welcomes me; and whoever welcomes me does not welcome me but the one who sent me.

Mark 9:37 NIV

Bruce wanted to be upright toward their dad, and be respectful of him.

The girls made the phone call to their biological dad (BD), and explained to him the desire of their heart. He was very gracious to them and said, "Well, girlies, if I had to hand-pick another daddy for you, it would be Bruce Bonner!" That was monumental! It was so wonderful of him, so big of him to say. It truly was a wonderful "God moment" for them. It was beautiful to see him put the girls' feelings first, before his own. I believe it caused them to be extra proud of their BD and love him all the more. He was able to be courageous in this moment, even in the face of something a bit fearful. This is what love is all about, putting others needs before yours and feeling really good about doing it right.

When we can get our egos and selfish desires out of the way, it surely is wonderful. God is able to do so much more through us and for us when we allow for it.

And he took the children in his arms, put his hands on them and blessed them.

Mark 10:16 NIV

Bruce carried them on his insurance, and paid for their entire upbringing. He has always been a man of peace and has always encouraged each of us to live accordingly. He's never had cross words with the girls' BD, only kindness towards him.

I'm not saying that being a blended family is easy. It's not. However, it can be done without fighting and bickering, even if you have the "right" to something. It doesn't mean that duking it out is going to solve anything. I believe that is what destroys. We should strive to make choices that create harmony and peace.

In order to do so, before you react out of anger, ask yourself, "Is this going to glorify God?" We are capable of stopping, taking a few deep breaths, and saying a prayer in order to focus on God rather than ourselves. The moment, the very moment that we take our focus off of God, that's when everything hits the fan. That's when you say things you regret, where all of the arguments start and seem to never end. It's where the constant states of tension and bitterness brew, creating hard hearts. I know, only because I've been guilty of it myself. It's not pretty.

As we age, we gain wisdom and insight from our past foolhardiness. If we don't learn from our prior mistakes, we continue perpetuating the same mistakes over and over; how ridiculous is that?! When we begin to glean insight, and recognize how we could have done things differently incorporating the positive change, we then perpetuate the positive growth and wisdom. Our failures are a huge part of our learning to be successful. It is here where God teaches us through our experiences our greatest life lessons. As I have looked back on what has transpired up to now, I see that all of it has propelled me to all I am doing and am about now in my life. It's all preparatory for God's calling upon my life. Rather than kicking ourselves, take the approach of what do I learn from this and being able to appreciate the learning. Oh, how wonderful it is to take this approach. Learning and growing and enjoying the process are paramount for us.

We have tried to model this kind of learning for our children, too. We admit where we are wrong (if we can see that we are wrong) and apologize for it, and explain in the apology what we learned in that situation. In the modeling of this, they grow from our mistakes, and learn that in their mistakes they are able to step back and find the growth points for themselves. In this way, tremendous burdens are lifted and no longer defeat us. This is where the victory can be found.

You may be divorced, or have had parents that were divorced, had a dear friend hurt you deeply, suffered the loss of a job or even deeper anguish where you wondered where God was. I have been there; I truly do understand what it's like to wonder if God cares, or if He was aware of me, my needs, my pain... There have times in my life where I didn't have understanding for years! In the process of simply moving forward, praying through it, I would ultimately have the hard conversations with the Lord and tell Him, I honestly do not feel Your presence with me, but I am *choosing* to trust You, to *believe* that You are with me, guiding me, directing me. Sometimes, years later, is when I would actually be able to trace the fingerprints of God, be able to see where the hand of God had been moving all the while. Trusting and believing God is where your faith builds, where the lessons are truly learned. This faith doesn't occur overnight, but it does day by day, step by faithful step.

Our daughters trusted their desire to call Bruce Dad. They trusted that their BD would be able to trust and not fear. The girls made a decision, and they talked it through with each other, then came to me and explained their desire. They never wanted harm for anyone.

> You will decide on a matter, and it will be established
> for you, and light will shine on your ways.
>
> Job 22:28 ESV

They were kind in their approach to him, and he in turn was kind to them. They were not trying to, nor would they ever want to replace him. Their BD didn't feel intimidated by their request; in fact he responded just the opposite, with love and respect. The girls approached their BD with honor and respect and were given the very same thing in return. It's amazing how they were able to teach me and their dads in this experience. Our children can teach us so much about love and the beauty of love; we just need to be open to the concept of being able to learn from them. *He speaks through our children—can you hear Him?* They are innocent and full of nothing but love in their innocence.

> Children's children are the crown of old men, and
> the glory of children is their fathers.
>
> Proverbs 17:6 TAB

# THE NAVAJO MISSION TRIP, WHO WAS IT REALLY FOR?

---

*The rivers appeared as though God simply engraved the place for the flowing streams to quench the thirst of the desert lands.*

---

*T*here in Navajoland, where the majestic red mountains stand tall and proud, there is a knowingness of the spiritual, and a sacred, Holy presence of God. It was a knowingness that was felt within my entire being.

On our mission trip to Navajoland, I was taken out of my typical everyday way of living. We brought our two daughters along who were at the beginning stages of societal influences. Any of you with children in middle school or high school, please feel free to sigh with exasperation right now! Boy, do I know those days! Taking our girls at this pivotal age was truly eye-opening for them. They came away with a new appreciation for what they had, and not so concerned with the material things they didn't have.

This was the first mission trip as a family, and it was while we were in seminary. We traveled to Navajoland just on the outskirts of Bluff, Utah. We took the trip with another seminary family, Robert and Julie Woody, along with their two sons, Seth and Sam. Robert is now ordained also and serving at a church in San Antonio. The eight of us packed our bags and headed out in Robert's dad's Suburban. The drive there was about twenty hours from Austin to Bluff and twenty hours back. The car ride there and back could be an entire chapter of deep belly laughs and poignant moments with our two families. We had such a great time.

*Something so foreign to me, and yet I recognized the sacredness of the song of the drum!*

We were partnering with St. Christopher's Episcopal Church in Navajoland on the outskirts of Bluff, across the San Juan River on the Navajo reservation. We called it "Navajoland." It is located in the spectacular red desert canyon, in the Four Corners area of Southeast Utah. We came to provide help with their Vacation Bible School for the Navajo children. The gentleman who was serving and living there was Episcopal Bishop Steven Plummer, a Navajo Indian himself, and the son of a medicine man. From what I recall he told us he'd lived all of his ordained life in Navajoland. He told us how he weaved together the Navajo and Episcopal traditions in ways that were sacred, experiential, spiritual, holy, and absolutely Divine. This is the place, on the Navajo reservation, where the church was centered, in which we were to do Vacation Bible School with the Navajo children who lived in Hogans surrounding the church.

The landscape was breathtaking and caused me to see and hear the majesty of God! The red rock cliffs and mountains were strong and rugged, yet majestic and graceful. The rivers appeared as though God simply engraved the place for the flowing streams to quench the thirst of the desert lands. If it were not for those rivers flowing through, it would appear as though the land were completely parched. The canyons are like the Lord carved His own cathedrals out of the rock. The beauty is striking; the cliffs soar straight up to the amazing sunsets which guide me directly to heaven!

> Out of the north he comes in golden splendor;
> God comes in awesome majesty.
>
> Job 37:22 NIV

The Navajo Reservation is alive here. I felt as though I could literally feel the heartbeat of the Navajo when I'd hear the beating drums in the distance. Like hearing rhythmic praises and prayers being lifted up to God. I imagined it 150 years ago as I stood there listening to the distant drumming. Oh, the visions it called upon in my spirit as I listened! Something so foreign to me, and yet I recognized the sacredness of the song of the drum! As I took in the landscape of the rugged, red rock canyons, I stood in awe of God's incredible design, witness to His splendor, His dramatic creation! The wonder of it all!

Let me understand the teaching of your precepts;
then I will meditate on your wonders.

Psalm 119:27 NIV

When we begin to contemplate going on a mission trip, I think we can sometimes allow our egos to lead us rather than Christ. I may be speaking more for myself than you; however I would imagine that many of you can relate. Sometimes, in our ego, we go there thinking that we have so much to teach those we are going to see. Thank God in His infinite wisdom He brings us back to reality and shows us the other side of the coin. He also sends us there to be taught! We are the ones who need to be opened up to another facet of His creation. Who is it that's really lost or misplaced? What are the teachings we are supposed to have? I love the way that the Lord uses the pull, tug, or nagging of others to get you to go where He wants you to go. You can be headed out on a mission for reasons you think are good, holy and sacred, going for the good of another, when you are the one in need of the awakening. I guess what I'm trying to say is to keep going on the mission trips you feel the pulling toward, go with an open mind of not feeling as though you have all the answers for those you are going to meet. Recognize that we always need to remain open and teachable; otherwise, I surmise that we will miss out on the miracle that is there for us and those we go to meet. I pray we don't.

> *Thank God in His infinite wisdom He brings us back to reality and shows us the other side of the coin.*

The Navajo we went to were Christian and didn't speak English. There is a depth in hearing the Lord's Prayer spoken in the Navajo language that I had not experienced before, nor have I since. While we were in Navajoland, I was given the blessed gift of hearing some Navajo children and a Navajo woman pray the Lord's Prayer in their native tongue. There is a strength that is so profound in the hearing of this prayer in their language; it was beautiful. As I stood there listening to them pray this prayer, it penetrated, sort of absorbed into my soul. It was a beholding that brought sacred tears to my eyes. It remains with me to this day.

※

The people there were poor compared to our average standards. On the other hand they themselves exhibited such richness, and so does the land they inhabit. The homes they lived in are called hogans. Let me share with you the little bit that I know in regard to their hogans! I was so struck by the primitive way in which they are built, not having any electricity or water, and yet they are built with such meaning and symbolism! They believe in building them in harmony with their beliefs. The roof is representative of the sky. The walls are representative of their surroundings, the upward mountains, and trees. The dirt floor is to be always in touch with the "earth mother." The size is small compared to the home in which most of us live. They are built of logs and mud.

The Hogans are octagonal houses, round as is the sun, with eight sides and four directions. The number four carries much symbolism in the Navajo traditions, signifying the four seasons, winter, spring, summer and fall, and the four directions, north, east, south, and west. They have the four sacred mountains, Mt. Taylor to the south, Mt. Blanca to the east, San Francisco Peak to the west, and Mt. Hesperus to the north, creating Navajoland.

The entrance to the hogan is required to face the east in order to catch the first rays of the morning light, and they believe the entrance door always brings honor and protection to the *Diyin Dineh* (the holy people). The stove is always in the center of the hogan, representing the sun of fire with a smoke hole in the center of the ceiling of the hogan. When the home is finished, the medicine man blesses the home with happiness from all directions, from the earth and the sky, with blessings of protection from illnesses and all things evil, with the promise of shelter to the family.

They have no water and no electricity. Their daily living was so different from mine. For me, in my daily living, I don't think about my home in terms of fundamental functions. I have the luxury of having a faucet in my kitchen, toilets and showers in the bathrooms; complete plumbing running through my home. I have electricity running through the walls of my home in which I insert plugs for curling irons, washer and dryers, stoves and refrigerators, blow dryers, computers, lamps, fish tanks, blenders, tea makers, night lights, oh, the list could go on and on. I don't ever have to think about where and when to gather water! I couldn't imagine planning my day around those things, and yet, here again, I might automatically see it as poverty. However, is God trying to slow me down in my hectic life? Should I take a new approach to the way I view this poverty, or shall I see the richness within? I might see it as my seeking the daily living water from my Lord. Oh, Lord, let me slow down enough each day so that I am always sure to drink daily from your living well!

*There is a depth in hearing the Lord's Prayer spoken in the Navajo language that I had not experienced before, nor have I since.*

Whoever believes in me, as the Scripture has said, streams of living water will flow from within him.

John 7:38 NIV

St. Christopher's church was one of the only places with a well for gathering water. They didn't charge the people for it. The people freely came each day to fill their big cans with water. We stayed in a house, a bed and breakfast not far from the reservation, that had water and electricity. At the close of each day, I pondered the events and was humbled by the Navajo people. I was awestruck by their fortitude, courage and strength and still am today. I would find myself wondering if they felt like they were in need, or if they enjoyed their simple lifestyle. In many ways I yearned for this kind of simplicity and oneness with nature. They didn't speak English so I was unable to ask the questions that would turn over in my head. I wanted to speak to them and ask them so much about the way they commune with God.

I know that many times God's voice can appear to be elusive and we can question if He longs to speak to us. There are times when you are in a place where you beg to hear something, anything at all from Him. I myself have often been in that very place of wondering. In reflection upon my states of desperation, I sense some of the major reasons that I wasn't able to hear Him, and when it seemed He was elusive to me it was because of my hectic lifestyle. We have so many things crammed in the daily calendar that our focus is on those "things" and not on the connection to God; therefore, we lose our connection to our Creator and oddly enough we wonder if He's present and question if God cares.

In my experience of allowing myself to wander off from God, out of "ear shot," I would venture to say that He's not going to be heard when I do that. If you and I don't take the time to get to know Him, we could miss Him completely. I personally believe that He is speaking to us all the time. However, if we don't take the time to cultivate a deep relationship with Him, then we fail to recognize His voice even when He is speaking to us. Therefore, we come to the false conclusion that He's not speaking to us. He could be trying so hard to have you hear Him, but you keep stuffing the day with things that are "more" important. We then wonder why it is that we never hear from Him while so many others do.

> *This is when there is no question about it; you know that you've heard Him speak, loudly, even in a whisper, straight into your heart.*

The Navajo taught me that they have the simplicity; they don't have the computers, the electricity, the water plumbed into their homes. They are able to stay connected to the things that truly matter. What do I stay connected to? What do I need to unplug?

Our girls, Tabitha and Kellie Ann, along with Robert and Julie's boys, Seth and Sam, were able to set aside the language barrier better than we adults could. It seems that playing games is one of those universal languages adults can seem to lose sight of. Tabitha said she was able to be more of herself, not worrying about clothing, but being loved and loving. They communicated through painting pictures, big smiles, and laughter, saying that they didn't need the English language to have a loving experience.

Each morning they would travel over the bumpy terrain in the big Suburban picking up the Navajo kids and bringing them to the church. The Navajo kids would jump inside the car without a word, just looking at you with their big, beautiful dark eyes. Once there at the church site, the singing, and the games began. We'd play kickball and hear laughter; we all know that laughter translates into fun! Oh, they loved kickball!

At the end of the day, they were driven back home in the same way; the only difference was the noise level. On the way home the chatter was bubbling, and so was the laughter. In the morning of the next day, again there was silence when they were picked up, and just as the day before, there was lots of bubbly chatter on the way home. Finally on the last two days, there wasn't nearly as much silence during the morning pick up. There was a relationship beginning to form, a trust being built, recognition. The relationships were being built due to the daily time being spent together. That's a beautiful thing, when love is seen, and felt and trusted.

This is true in our relationship with God. As we spend time with Him in His Word, in continual study, we begin to get to know Him on a level that has depth, causing us to know His character. This is when we begin to hear Him speak. This is when there is no question about it; you know that you've heard Him speak, loudly, even in a whisper, straight into your heart. For me, most of the time, God doesn't speak into my ears; but directly into my heart or directly into my mind and soul. He does this by various means, by using other people to speak truth into me. By having a word in the Scripture jump out at me, having a passage of Scripture cause me to be renewed and transform my mind. By way of music, songs of praise and worship, through the beating of a drum in the distant, Navajoland sky.

At this my heart pounds and leaps from its place. Listen! Listen to the roar of his voice, to the rumbling that comes from his mouth. He unleashes his lightning beneath the whole heaven and sends it to the ends of the earth. After that comes the sound of his roar; he thunders with his majestic voice. When his voice resounds, he holds nothing back. God's voice thunders in marvelous ways; he does great things beyond our understanding.

Job 37:1–5 NIV

> *In my reflection of profound moments in my life;*
> *they stay with me, they remain as brilliantly lit*
> *memories, and I believe that when we've been struck*
> *with that kind of light, it remains lit in the minds*
> *and hearts of those that were there who felt it too.*

Oh, how my heart beats, how it pounds when I hear Him! His works are amazing! I long to have at least a piece of the Navajo way remain a part of my beating heart. So how do we extract the parallels in our own lives within the context of what we have learned while there? What can I take back with me, what learning, what can be implemented? What part of it can I hold inside, to remain as a part of who I am now, after this experience has brought about some sort of transformation within? Are there any pieces of my Spirit that have touched them the way that theirs has touched me? One likes to think so, but one doesn't always know. I am one to believe that in my reflection of profound moments in my life; they stay with me, they remain as brilliantly lit memories, and I believe that when we've been struck with that kind of light, it remains lit in the minds and hearts of those that were there who felt it too. It certainly does for me! I think this is one of the ways He does great things within us beyond our understanding!

I'm thankful that this mission trip remains with me today. It lives within me, remains lit! God, I pray that the pieces of clarity you provide me in the amazing ways that you do, would spill over somehow. That I would do with it and all the other experiences you provide me what you want me to do with them. Let me be a faithful steward of the lessons. Let me be broadened horizontally and vertically in my mind, heart and spirit! Let me never be arrogant when you have me go, but always open to hear what it is you want me to learn, to be teachable, and love all people no matter their culture and differences.

Do you want to hear Him? Do you want to know when it is that He's speaking to you? Do you have this as one of your greatest desires of your life? I do. I do every day! If you do, then let us make the time. Let us walk daily to the well, step out in service, away from the phones, the TV's, and the things that keep us pulled away from Him. Take the time to go on the mission trips, if it's what God would have you do. Should you go beyond your own backyard for mission work? Yes, absolutely, if it's where He's calling you! There is something amazing that happens deep within your soul that words can not express. It's deep connection from your spirit to another, where the Holy Spirit dwelling within you connects with the Holy Spirit in another. There are no deeper levels of connection when this happens! Of course, you don't have to go far away to experience this kind of connection. Is this the only way to live into this kind of profoundness? No, absolutely not! We have mission work to be done right here in our own backyards, in our own neighborhoods, in our very own hearts.

Unplug and go to the well...

Oh Lord, let me seek You with a reverence, with a trust so big! Let me hear You in all peoples, see You in all peoples. Lord, I can fall so short... and I come to You again and again with the hope of who I am to be. Lord, let me see all people, all cultures with wide- eyed curiosity and profound love! Lord, let them teach me what You'd have me to learn. I come before You with the hope of who You are creating me to be. I have a "knowing" of who You are creating me to be and a profound yearning to be that creation now, though I recognize I am still in the process of this intense journey with You. Amen

In special recognition of the Navajo Code Talkers in service to our country during World War II, I'd like to honor them with the following excerpt...

For Immediate Release
Office of the Press Secretary
July 26, 2001

*Remarks by the President in a Ceremony Honoring the Navajo Code Talkers*
Rotunda, U.S. Capitol Washington, D.C.
1:41 p.m. EDT

THE PRESIDENT: Thank you very much. Today, America honors 21 Native Americans who, in a desperate hour, gave their country a service only they could give. In war, using their native language, they relayed secret messages that turned the course of battle. At home, they carried for decades the secret of their own heroism. Today, we give these exceptional Marines the recognition they earned so long ago.

I want to thank the Congress for inviting me here, Mr. Speaker. I want to thank Senators Campbell, Bingaman and Johnson and Congressman Udall for their leadership. I want to thank Sergeant Major McMichael, distinguished guests, ladies and gentlemen, welcome to Washington, D.C.

The gentlemen with us, John Brown, Chester Nez, Lloyd Oliver, Allen Dale June and Joe Palmer, represented by his son Kermit, are the last of the original Navajo Code Talkers. In presenting gold medals to each of them, the Congress recognizes their individual service, bravely offered and flawlessly performed.

With silver medals, we also honor the dozens more who served later, with the same courage and distinction. And with all these honors, America pays tribute to the tradition and community that produced such men, the great Navajo Nation. The paintings in this rotunda tell of America and its rise as a nation. Among them are images of the first Europeans to reach the coast, and the first explorer to come upon the Mississippi.

But before all these firsts on this continent, there were the first people. They are depicted in the background, as if extras in the story. Yet, their own presence here in America predates all human record. Before others arrived, the story was theirs alone.

Today we mark a moment of shared history and shared victory. We recall a story that all Americans can celebrate, and every American should know. It is a story of ancient people, called to serve in a modern war. It is a story of one unbreakable oral code of the Second World War, messages traveling by field radio on Iwo Jima in the very language heard across the Colorado plateau centuries ago.

Above all, it's a story of young Navajos who brought honor to their nation and victory to their country. Some of the Code Talkers were very young, like Albert Smith, who joined the Marines at 15. In order to enlist, he said, I had to advance my age a little bit. At least one Code Talker was over-age, so he claimed to be younger in order to serve. On active duty, their value was so great, and their order so sensitive, that they were closely guarded. By war's end, some 400 Navajos had served as Code Talkers. Thirteen were killed in action, and their names, too, are on today's roll of honor.

Regardless of circumstances, regardless of history, they came forward to serve America. The Navajo code itself provides a part of the reason. Late in his life, Albert Smith explained, the code word for America was, "Our Mother." Our Mother stood for freedom, our religion, our ways of life, and that's why we went in. The Code Talkers joined 44,000 Native Americans who wore the uniform in World War II. More than 12,000 Native Americans fought in World War I. Thousands more served in Korea, Vietnam and serve to this very day.

Twenty-four Native Americans have earned the highest military distinction of all, the Medal of Honor, including Ernest Childers, who was my guest at the White House last week. In all these wars and conflicts, Native Americans have served with the modesty and strength and quiet valor their tradition has always inspired.

That tradition found full expression in the Code Talkers, in those absent, and in those with us today. Gentlemen, your service inspires the respect and admiration of all Americans, and our gratitude is expressed for all time, in the medals it is now my honor to present.

May God bless you all. (Applause.)

(The medals are presented.) (Applause.)

END 1:48 p.m. EDT

Please know that we praise God for you and your service to a country that was not honoring you at that time. Your grace is huge, and so is your spirit.

# KNOWING GOD THROUGH THE STUDY OF HIS WORD

---

*How does one come to love the Lord God with all of his or her heart, soul, and mind?*

---

"Teacher, which is the greatest commandment in the Law?" Jesus replied: "'Love the Lord your God with all your heart and with all your soul and with all your mind. This is the first and greatest commandment. And the second is like it: 'Love your neighbor as yourself. All the Law and the Prophets hang on these two commandments."

Matthew 22:36–40 NIV

How does one come to love the Lord God with all of his or her heart, soul, and mind? In my experience it is through the study of His Word. This is how we come to know Him, revere Him, respect Him, follow Him, trust Him and truly love Him. Through the study of the God-breathed pages, we cannot help but love Him with all of our heart, with all of our soul, and with our entire mind. It becomes a natural outpouring, the natural expression of love, by spending that kind of time with Him and getting to know Him thoroughly. This is true intimacy with God.

Permit me to share with you a small splash of some passages that speak further into who He is. Enjoy these passages; meditate on them. Explore your thoughts surrounding a few of these; witness His majesty revealed here as you begin to get a glimpse of our Lord God's multiple facets...

> Do you know how God controls the clouds and makes his lightning flash?
>
> Job 37:15 NIV

> Do you not know? Have you not heard? The LORD is the everlasting God, the Creator of the ends of the earth. He will not grow tired or weary, and his understanding no one can fathom.
>
> Isaiah 40:28 NIV

> All Scripture is God-breathed...
>
> 2 Timothy 3:16 NIV

> I know that everything God does will endure forever; nothing can be added to it and nothing taken from it. God does it so that men will revere him.
>
> Ecclesiastes 3:14 NIV

"Ask in my name, according to my will, and he'll most certainly give it to you. Your joy will be a river overflowing its banks!"

John 16:24 MSG

God formed man out of dirt from the ground and blew into his nostrils the breath of life! The man came alive—a living soul!

Genesis 2:7 MSG

*I was not nor have I ever been let down in my pursuit of knowing Him.*

"Be still, and know that I am God; I will be exalted among the nations, I will be exalted in the earth."

Psalm 46:10 NIV

God made two great lights—the greater light to govern the day and the lesser light to govern the night. He also made the stars.

Genesis 1:16 NIV

O LORD, you have searched me and you know me. You know when I sit and when I rise; you perceive my thoughts from afar. You discern my going out and my lying down; you are familiar with all my ways. Before a word is on my tongue you know it completely, O LORD. You hem me in—behind and before; you have laid your hand upon me. Such knowledge is too wonderful for me, too lofty for me to attain. Where can I go from your Spirit? Where can I flee from your presence? If I go up to the heavens, you are there; if I make my bed in the depths, you are there. If I rise on the wings of the dawn, if I settle on the far side of the sea, 0 even there your hand will guide me, your right hand will hold me fast. If I say, "Surely the darkness will hide me and the light become night around me," even the darkness will not be dark to you; the night will shine like the day, for darkness is as light to you. For you created my inmost being; you knit me together in my mother's womb. I praise you because I am fearfully and wonderfully made; your works are wonderful, I know that full well. My frame was not hidden from you when I was made in the secret place. When I was woven together in the depths of the earth, your eyes saw my unformed body. All the days ordained for me were written in your book before one of them came to be. How precious to me are your thoughts, O God! How vast is the sum of them!

Psalm 139: 1–17 NIV

In my growing up years, my mom and dad took us to church regularly. I don't recall us missing a Sunday. We enjoyed going to church, and my brothers and sister and I all believe in God. We went to Sunday school classes each week and learned the many Bible characters and stories. As we got older something changed in the way that we were learning. I can't recall what it was exactly that caused the change. However, I do know the divorce of my parents, the shifting, and cracking that inevitably occurs with such a break in the family, the wrong choices I made as a result were major contributors. I can't help but think it had to do with my desire to be cool. Whatever the cause, I seemed to receive less and less of the foundation of the Word being poured into and over me during those crucial, adolescent growing up years.

I believed in God, yes absolutely, unequivocally, without any doubt, as did my siblings and my parents and most of my friends. The question isn't or wasn't did I believe in God; the question for me was, and the one that I'll pose to you now is, do I know God, do I REALLY know God? Who are you, God? The answer for me was what shook me a bit; it was NO, I don't really know God, but I seemed only to know *of* God! Wow! What a realization this was for me; because I professed to be one who believed in Him, I would NEVER have said that I didn't believe in God! So how is it that I support that belief? With these thoughts and questions running rampant in my head, I began to feel the need to find out who God was.

> *How do I get to know God; how do I get to know Him well?*

Upon that realization that I really didn't know Him well, I had to ask the next question, how? How do I get to know God; how do I get to know Him well? I thought, further reassuring myself that I did have a sense of familiarity of Him. Then questioning if I felt that I had a familiarity with Him because of my study of His Word or was it through others that knew Him? I realized there was a big difference! Many times I can form opinions of someone I do not know through the opinion of someone else when I have had no personal experience with them. I'm sure that many of you can relate. That formed opinion based on someone else's experience isn't always correct. I can not truly know that person, judge that person, or be in any kind of true and honest relationship with them based on somebody else's opinion. There is a big difference. I hadn't done any in-depth study of His Word, and yet I formed strong opinions and beliefs on things. I have always been one to believe that I shouldn't form opinions about someone based on another's opinion. I need to be able to form my own relationships with folks based on my own experiences with them.

After studying the Word for many years, I discovered that I was of the opinion that there were basically two different Gods, one of the Old Testament (whom I didn't think I would like and viewed Him as an explosive angry God) and one of the New Testament (whom I thought was a nicer God, and therefore I would be more inclined to like this God)! I've met many folks who have had similar thoughts and opinions. What I've learned through this type of blundered practice is that one cannot know someone without being in relationship with them. We can not know the heart of anyone if we have not been in connection with them. Yes, we can know them to some degree, and we can hear others' thoughts and opinions about them; we can be acquainted with certain things and form assessments based on the bits and pieces of information we have. One needs to know a person well before they can establish sound opinions, beliefs and judgments about them.

When I began to attempt to study the Bible fifteen years ago, I was yearning to know God and yet was frustrated with my inability to decipher the symbolism in the parables, and my lack of historical knowledge kept me from understanding what I so desperately wanted to understand. The Bible is deep, profound and rich with wisdom for each of us. In the beginning of your study it can seem overwhelming; however, do not allow that to stop you! I tell you this because I remember those times of thinking that I was never going to get it. Even finding your way from one chapter to the next is daunting, and you can feel embarrassed that you don't know where the different books of the Bible are located. Please don't let that stop you; we all have been there, we all have to start somewhere.

*For those of you who like to look like your are in control, this will be a good time to let God be in control, become humble in your discovery of His majesty.*

The parables can be difficult to make heads or tails of when we don't understand the culture of the day, therefore, failing to make any sense to us when reading.

This can cause frustration; the thoughts that occurred to me were things like, *"This makes no sense," "This is way over my head," "I'm never going to understand this,"* which would cause me to give up trying. Many times I had thoughts that it was impossible to glean any kind of insight and wondered if I would ever have any kind of understanding.

This is where you need to let your ego go and realize that each person in the room started out not knowing much of anything. For those of you who like to look like you are in control, this will be a good time to let God be in control, become humble in your discovery of His majesty.

I'm not sharing all of this with you to scare you, but to assure you that each of us who get to know our Lord through His glorious Word share the same beginning frustrations. I want to be an encourager for you to press on! It's worth it. Oh, is it ever worth it! I am not trying to make it appear as though I am a Bible scholar either, and don't want it to appear that I know all there is to know by any means. I have so much more to learn! The more I learn, the more I realize that there is so much more for me to discover about Christ and about myself in Christ! What I can tell you is that it becomes easier, richer, and actually begins to make sense. To have the Word poured into your heart and move you to places you never thought were possible is truly living! This is what it means when it is called the Living Word. Is it ever!

> For the word of God is living and active. Sharper than any double-edged sword, it penetrates even to

dividing soul and spirit, joints and marrow; it judges the thoughts and attitudes of the heart.

Hebrews 4:12 NIV

Pray that the Lord would grant you wisdom and insight and make His ways known to you, that you would be given the insights into His will for you, and you will be granted it. The Lord will reveal! He loves to reveal Himself to us! You will love what you find!

Being deeply rooted in a great Bible study is crucial, and I personally have to recommend Bible Study Fellowship to you. A friend of mine invited me to join her in classes there. This gift of invitation was, and remains to this day, one of the most precious gifts I have ever been given. The blessings of this gift remain with me today. I had never heard of BSF, and only knew the bit of information she gave me, that it was a nation-wide Bible study, and that they met weekly, and it was FREE! I accepted her invitation, and went to the intro class. I listened to the presenter as she explained the details of BSF and how they worked, the objectives, the vision, the purpose. I stayed for the lecture afterward. Then found myself signing up to be placed in a class with the hope and anticipation that there would be an opening available. They assured me that they would call me when there was an opening.

> *The more I learn, the more I realize that there is so much more for me to discover about Christ and about myself in Christ!*

This invitation to BSF changed my life! I want to present you with the very same invitation! Find a BSF near you, and get started! This is one of the greatest gifts that has ever been given to me! It is the gift that keeps on giving!

As I began with the classes, I was humbled and thrilled to be in the study of the Word. I began my exploration into the wonderment of who God was and is today by going each and every week to my BSF classes. This is such a wonderful place for you to start your in-depth study, and exploration into the heart of God! The study is free, which is amazing because of all of the printed notes that are provided to each student, each week around the world! BSF is open to all denominations.

I went all seven years, and six of those years I was a discussion leader. Each class is full of many different denominations. BSF never discusses denomination in the class; it is focused completely on the Word, bringing about a unity of the people with no divisions regarding denominations. That is a wonderful thing! I am encouraging you to come before the Lord, opening His Word with an open heart, an open mind, and leave your ego out of it. I would encourage you to come at it with an explorer's heart, with the idea of discovery, sort of like a treasure hunter!

As you become one who is hunting for treasure within the Word, you will find answers, and more questions, oodles of wisdom, rebirth, love, truth, joy, kindness, a deeper faith, compassion, fervor for life, and so much more! All of which are priceless jewels that you can pass down to your children as a bountiful inheritance. These are the things that are of value, that you can put your trust. You will find the things of your heart that bring the great promises to your life!

When I began the study of the Word of God, I went *wanting to know* God, *wanting to find* Him, and with a *huge desire to experience* Him, to be in a relationship with Him! I wanted to have Him engrained in me, be a part of who I am. I wanted to have Him be my Master and my Guide, to be my Counselor, my Healer, my Love! The yearning was great, and I was not nor have I ever been let down in my pursuit of knowing Him through the study of His written Word. My faith gets bigger with it, and I know yours will also as He reveals Himself to you.

For any relationship for it to be healthy, deep, and real, commitment is required. The study of His Word takes commitment! I want to talk to you about commitment and what that word means. The dictionary defines commitment as: *The act of committing. The state of being committed. The act of pledging, or engaging oneself. A pledge or promise; obligation.* When you commit yourself to the study, you will experience a new life in Him, one that can not be matched with how your life was before.

*I would encourage you to come at it with an explorer's heart, with the idea of discovery, sort of like a treasure hunter!*

When I come to Him, when I begin to open the pages of my Bible, I find words that jump out at me; I circle them, journal them, study them, discover the meaning behind them. Ask the Lord to reveal to you what He wants you to learn. He does and He always will!

Through BSF, the continual study through all seven years, the commitment I made to come to the classes is how I committed to staying in His Holy Word, and through His Holy Word I know God deeply, intimately. I found out about His character, His nature, His truth, His majesty, that He is the God of second and third and fourth... chances. I found forgiveness for all of my messes, which He has turned into a glorious message for Him; I found out what grace is; I discovered His astonishing love for me!

Do you have a desire to know God and to love God? Let me recommend BSF to you or Precepts, or CBS (Community Bible Study). All of these are fantastic, indepth studies.

As a discussion leader in BSF, the Lord used that time for me to be groomed in leadership, and I was able to learn homiletics as well. Go to His Word, find your God and find who you are in Him; I promise you will never ever regret it!

# THE BUG TRUCK

---
✳
---

> *It is in times like these that we utilize the*
> *"gift of humor" as we press through the mundane*
> *and irritating situations of "teenage-hood,"*
> *and boy, do we ever applaud God for this most*
> *wonderful gift of humor!*

*M*om, can you take me to school? Melissa isn't going to be able to take me today!"

Tabby hollers up the stairs as I am rushing to finish getting ready and head out the door to work. I can feel the tension build in me and the frustration rising immediately. I holler back, "Tabitha, you need to tell me these things the night before, so that we can plan for it, I'm already running late!"

"*Mom!* I didn't know last night, Melissa *just now* called me, and so I'm telling you *now!*"

"Well, *why* didn't Melissa call last night? Why is she *just* now letting you know this?!"

"How should I know!? Maybe she just found out. All I know is that I need a ride to school. Can you *please, please* take me? *Please*, Mom?!"

Kellie Ann jumps in at her sister's defense. "Mom, Melissa really did just now call, she's not lying; I am the one who answered the phone!"

I holler back, "I'm not accusing her of lying!"

"Well, excuse me!" Kellie Ann says.

I look at Bruce with a bit of frustration, and he just shrugs his shoulder and shakes his head, obviously not wanting to get in on the chaos.

I imagine Tabitha thanks Kellie Ann for the save, giving her a big high five. They stand united as the sisterhood prevails!

"Tabitha, I have a meeting that I cannot be late for! I have to be there early, because I'm the one leading the meeting! There is no way I can get you to school and get to my meeting on time, absolutely no way! Can you catch the bus?"

"Uhh! No, mom, I don't *want* to ride the bus! Besides, the bus came a long time ago!"

I turn to Bruce, "Hon, what's your schedule like today? Can you take her?"

"Yeah, it's going to push it a bit for me, but I can do it. We need to leave in the next ten minutes, though; you think she can be ready by then?"

> *Oh, let us never ever put out*
> *the Spirit's fire!*

"She's going to *have* to be ready by then, won't she? Are you going to be in the car, or do you have to take the bug truck today?"

"I'll be in the bug truck," he says with a funny look on his face.

"Do you have time to take them in the car then come back and get the bug truck afterward?" I ask trying to alleviate the upcoming frustration of her having to ride in the bug truck.

"No, I can't; this is already going to really be pushing it for me as it is."

"Okay, I'll go tell them to hurry. Thanks, Hon."

We both know how completely devastating the bug truck can be to someone of her stature! How dare we even think that her highness should ever grace that lowly truck with her presence! We both look at each other and start to giggle, thanking God that she is not near us to see the kind of twisted delight we are getting from the thought of it. Certainly God gives us a sense of humor, doesn't He? It is in times like these that we utilize the "gift of humor" as we press through the mundane and irritating situations of "teenage-hood," and boy, do we ever applaud God for this most wonderful gift of humor!

On your feet now—applaud God! Bring a gift of laughter, sing yourselves into his presence.

Psalm 100:1 MSG

So... we now began to brace ourselves with the armor of God before we have to let her know that she's going to be riding in the bug truck! We huddle up, shoot up a quick prayer under our breath... chuckle real good and head into the *teenage danger zone,* knowing full well the battle we are about to face...

I proceed downstairs with my armor in place in order to dodge the flying arrows headed straight at my mind and heart. I am protected! I talk to myself, reminding myself that I will not be defeated emotionally by a teenager, as I continue to wear my smile. I slowly and cautiously approach the girls to let them know that I can't take them, and that they are in luck: Dad will be able to. I stand waiting for them to cheer with joy that we have come up a way to make it happen! Both of them look at each other, sending some sort of teenage waves of ESP; somehow they know that the bug truck is going to be employed in their morning journey to school. Somehow my ESP has kicked in as well, as I am aware of what they are thinking and what they are on the verge of saying! Here we go... I'm going in, reminding myself again that I am protected, and will not be defeated by teenagers!

"Girls, because of my meeting I can't take you; Dad's got the extra time and he's happy to do it."

*Are you viewing things in a perspective that brings about growth and learning, or do you need to shift your perspective a bit?*

Kellie Ann looks to her big sister, and it's as though she's prompting her to ask about the bug truck and what involvement it may have.

Of course, Tabitha reads her mind and is wondering the very same thing herself. She looks at me with a frown so big (the kind only a mother could love) and asks, "Are we going in the car?"

"No, Dad's got work before seminary, so it's going to be the bug truck." I say this bracing myself for the demoralizing response sure to come my way... all the while secretly wishing that her response would be "Oh, that's okay. I'm just glad he can take me," with a beautiful, heartfelt smile...

Back to reality I come. Both Tabitha and Kellie Ann look at each other and their eyes roll, and the heavy winds from a huge huff of irritation come blowing straight at me, saying, "Oh! I hate that bug truck!"

Tabitha hollers upstairs, "Dad, is there *any* possible way you can take us in the car *first* and then come back to the house and switch to the bug truck?"

"No, honey, I can't," he says.

"*Pleeease,* Dad!"

"No, honey, I really can't. I don't have that kind of time on my hands. We need to get movin'; we need to be out the door in five minutes in order for me to get to the places I need to get to on time; let's get going."

"*Five minutes!* I don't think I can be ready that soon! Dad!! I *hate* that bug truck! It's so *embarrassing!*" Tabitha says, exasperated.

"The more you stand around here complaining the more time you're wasting; let's get going honey," Bruce says.

Then under his breath I hear him say, "You're welcome."

"Well, just drop me off two blocks from the school so no one sees me get out of that truck!" Tabitha demands.

The "teenage huff" is heard as she rushes off to get ready and climb into the stinky, chemical-smelling bug truck.

> *When you feel as though you have been marred, some by your own doing or some by others, climb into His hands.*

Somehow over the course of time our kids became too cool to ride the bus. We don't know why it happened, or how it happened, it just sort of became *uncool* to be a bus rider. The bus was reliable, always on time, always picked them up in the very same spot and always got them to their destination. We didn't have to worry about how they'd get to the bus stop as it was just three houses down.

I loved riding the bus when I was her age! I have some of the fondest memories of laughing with my friends at the bus stop and on the bus. Walking home with friends, it truly was a wonderful time. All kinds of exciting conversations were to be heard. Homework was even done on the bus, leaving us with the rest of the afternoon to play!

Why is it that we as parents feel the need to apologize because we don't provide a chariot for the kids to ride in? How is it that we don't get showered with hugs and kisses and many thanks for the shifting of our hectic schedules? Why must there be those typical teenage huffs? Because that's the way God made teenagers, especially teenage girls! It is through this journey of raising our kids that He is speaking to us; and teaching us how to give, to love, and growing our character as adults, causing us to lean on Him all the more. It grants us the chance to create teachable moments for our children. It affords us the opportunity to educate them to value and honor us as their parents.

The girls got to school, and were *not* dropped off two blocks away. They were dropped off in front of the school, and no one said a word to them about it; they were oblivious to it. It's funny how we can get so caught up in worrying about what others are thinking or what others are going to say.

From time to time if they were misbehaving, we would threaten to take them to school in the bug truck if they didn't straighten up! It got their attention, and provided us with a good giggle!

I personally was grateful to everything the bug truck represented to our household. It was during seminary that Bruce took on the part time job as an exterminator. We were in need of the extra income as money was so tight; we had teenage girls who had needs as well as wants that we wanted to provide them. Besides that, we had bills to pay, and financially we needed the extra income.

Isn't it funny... interesting how we can perceive the very same thing so differently? Bruce and I saw the bug truck as such a bountiful blessing. At the very same time, the girls saw it as such an embarrassment, a curse if you will. The way each of us view things in our lives is key.

So much of life is truly about the perspective from which we view it. I know that it can seem like a cliché statement; however, it has a powerful effect in our lives. The Lord has given us the power of choice, and we always stand in the freedom of choice. The Word tells us to give thanks in all circumstances.

> Be joyful always, pray continually, and give thanks in all circumstances, for this is God's will for you in Christ Jesus. Do not put out the Spirit's fire...
>
> 1 Thessalonians 5:16–19 NIV

And I don't think the word ALL means selective; I think it means in *all* things. Be joyful! Rejoice in whatever you have, rather than cursing it and seeing it as something that is not good, but see it as goodness that provides because He is the great provider. If you feel like the car you have is not good enough, you fail to see the blessing that you have been given, you are putting out the Spirit's fire!

Oh, let us *never* ever put out the Spirit's fire! Let us never become complacent or ignorant at the way the Holy Spirit is at work in our lives. Let us never become complacent in our way of approaching our work, our worship, our daily living. Let us always radiate that Holy glow and share in the warmth of this Holy glow!

We can look at so many of the circumstances in our lives as a burden rather than a blessing. Many times when those things that seem as though they are a burden, they are the gift of character building, trust building, hope building, bridges in your faith.

We choose at all times what kind of perspective we stand in. Let's take a closer look at the two perspectives we have and the way they can filter them into our daily living. "Being cursed" is the first perspective and the second perspective of "being blessed." If I view the bug truck as a curse or something that is not good, I fail to experience pride in my husband for providing. If I had seen it as not good, my husband would not have felt valued by me. If Bruce saw it a something that was not good, he could have seen the job as an irritation, and therefore been frustrated and unhappy. This would also cause him to fail to glean the insights for pastoral care that the Lord had for him to learn during this time. The additional income that we had was such a benefit for us as well. It was good, hard work that also gave reprieve to the daily seminary studies.

Are you viewing things in a perspective that brings about growth and learning, or do you need to shift your perspective a bit? Think about any given situation or challenge, do you view it as an opportunity or as a burden? God is always about growing us, giving us new ways to function, new insight into the way we live our lives. In what situation can you shift the view from a curse to a blessing? Look for the blessings from God, not the curses, and your entire life will begin to take on new shape, your focus no longer blurred, but bright and clear.

In all fairness to the girls, they were great kids and really didn't ask for much. They were grateful for all that they had, and have told me that they really never knew how financially stretched we were. I am so thankful that they never knew how extended we were. We can only praise God for that.

The job Bruce took as an exterminator was ministry. Every occupation, every trade, every job is. Not only does it provide income, it also provides opportunity for each of us to be in relationship with God and all His people.

Each job we have whether it is a temporary position or something we do as a life-long career is a time of growth, and adding tools to our tool kit. It is a sense of giving and receiving that goes on. We give our best to the folks we serve and receive blessings because of it. We hone our skills as leaders as we learn to handle the many personalities we encounter along the way. As we love with the love of Christ in our serving at work, we love what we do! It's the relationships that make the difference in all that we do. Care for each person you come in contact with, look at them the way Christ would, bring more meaning into your everyday work.

Bruce had some ghastly tasks as a pest control exterminator, and he says it was some of the finest ministry training he ever got! He learned such a great deal as he crawled around in the sweltering, hot attics searching for rodents. The people he was serving had a need; they wanted help in solving a problem. Many times these critters were dreadfully scary to them. They were filled with anxiety and full of hope in what the pest control company could accomplish. Bruce says this job actually taught him pastoral care because he learned how to help people with their problems. You might find this interesting and wonder how that would be true. As he helped solve or eradicate an ant problem or a roach problem, he was able to contribute to making their lives so much better. He learned how to talk to people with compassion. Because he had a pest control uniform and a pest control truck, he was invited into their home, and often times invited briefly into their lives. Sometimes they would open up to him about a current problem they were facing. It helped him to learn to listen. He took much of what he learned with him into his ministry.

Each job we have along the way provides us new and fresh experiences in life. It is part of the molding and the shaping by God. He wants to shape us into vessels of service.

> If anyone serves, he should do it with the strength God provides, so that in all things God may be praised through Jesus Christ.
>
> 1 Peter 4:11 NIV

Take the journey to the Potter's house, and allow the Lord to use His loving hands to mold and shape you, right where you are. Step willingly into His hands.

> This is the word that came to Jeremiah from the LORD: "Go down to the Potter's house and there I will give you my message." So I went to the Potter's house, and I saw Him working at His wheel. But the pot he was shaping from the clay was marred in His hands; so the Potter formed it into another pot, shaping it as seemed best to Him. Then the word of the LORD came to me...
>
> Jeremiah 18:1–5 NIV

> *Take the journey to the Potter's house, and allow*
> *the Lord to use His loving hands to mold and*
> *shape you, right where you are. Step willingly*
> *into His hands.*

In all the different roles you enter into throughout the course of your life, the Lord uses all of those things and all of those moments to speak into your life, to shape you into a beautiful creation. When you feel as though you have been marred, some by your own doing or some by others, climb into His hands. He is always able to rework us, reshape us into a work of art. No matter the work you do, whether it is of slight income or extreme income, whether it is a job you are not fond of or a job in which you love, allow yourself to find Him in the work and in the people. You will hear Him in the most incredible ways if you keep your ears and heart open to hear. *Shhhh, listen! Can you hear Him? He is speaking!*

So, whether your chariot is a bug truck or a Ferrari; enjoy the journey, and give thanks to God!

Give thanks to the LORD, for He is good; His love endures forever.

1 Chronicles 16:34 NIV

# OPPORTUNITIES TO DONATE
## TO WORTHY CAUSES

For opportunities to serve or contribute to causes that are near and dear to the author's heart, go to the following websites:

*Apartment Life* is a non-profit 501(c)3 organization and is unique as a ministry in that over 90% of their expenses are covered by operating revenue, and their goal over the next few years is to be financially self-sufficient. Until that time, the CARES Program depends on the financial gifts of individuals and churches. Without this support, the teams would be unable to change the world through CARES. To give go to www.CaresTeam.org or www.ApartmentLife.org and click on "Donate".

*New Beginnings Mentoring Ministry* is a non-profit 501(c)3 organization and group of individuals and community sponsors that are determined to give single moms, who are seeking a better life, a chance to keep their families together by providing that little extra something they need. Those needs are as simple as pointing to the right resources in the community. Some needs are met on a more involved basis: babysitting, encouragement, job search assistance, parenting training… the list goes on. Without someone to help provide necessary resources, some single moms are faced with giving up educational, vocational, or career training opportunities in order to keep and provide for their children. We empower each single mother, who finds herself facing these overwhelming challenges, to pursue her path to a better life while keeping her young family together. To donate or provide support go to www.NewBeginningsMM.org and click on "Donate Online."

*For more information, please visit*

WWW.KATHRYNBONNER.COM